JAMES G. HUDKINS JR
FEB 2017 -
HAMILTON

CADWALLADER COLDEN

CADWALLADER COLDEN
A Biography

SEYMOUR I. SCHWARTZ

Humanity Books

an imprint of Prometheus Books
59 John Glenn Drive, Amherst, New York 14228-2119

Published 2013 by Humanity Books, an imprint of Prometheus Books

Cover design by Liz Scinta

Inquiries should be addressed to
Humanity Books
59 John Glenn Drive
Amherst, New York 14228–2119
VOICE: 716–691–0133
FAX: 716–691–0137
WWW.PROMETHEUSBOOKS.COM

17 16 15 14 13   5 4 3 2 1

Library of Congress Cataloging-in-Publication Data

Schwartz, Seymour I., 1928-
    Cadwallader Colden : a biography / by Seymour I. Schwartz.
        pages cm
    Includes bibliographical references and index.
    ISBN 978-1-61614-853-9 (hardback)
    ISBN 978-1-61614-854-6 (ebook)
    1. Colden, Cadwallader, 1688-1776. 2. Lieutenant governors—New York (State)—Biography. 3. New York (State)—History—Colonial period, ca. 1600-1775—Biography. 4. United States—History—Colonial period, ca. 1600-1775—Biography. 5. New York (State)—Intellectual life—18th century. 6. United States—Intellectual life—18th century. 7. Intellectuals—United States—Biography. 8. Scientists—United States—Biography. 9. Royalists—United States—Biography. I. Title.

F122.C6872 2013
973.2—dc23

                                                    2013028690

Printed in the United States of America

CONTENTS

ACKNOWLEDGMENTS

To Dennis Carr, a staff member of the Miner Library of the University of Rochester Medical Center, whose assistance over the past several years was invaluable. To Gianna Nixon for her graphic assistance.

ℰℰ INTRODUCTION ℰℰ

*T*he second half of the year of 1776 witnessed several historic events in British Colonial North America. On July 2, the thirteen colonies declared their independence from Great Britain. Two days later, the Declaration of Independence was adopted by the Congress in Philadelphia. On the same day, the British fleet was sighted off New York. On September 15, the British occupied the City of New York, which George Washington and his army had just abandoned, moving north to encamp at Harlem Heights. On September 21, about one-third of lower Manhattan was destroyed by the Great New York Fire of 1776. Also on September 21, Nathan Hale, a spy in the Continental Army, was captured near Flushing Bay in Queens, New York, behind enemy lines. He was hanged the next day at the Park of Artillery (current 66th Street and Third Avenue in Manhattan). Nathan Hale was immortalized by the statement he issued before the hanging: "I only regret that I have but one life to give for my country." On the day before Nathan Hale's capture, also in Flushing, not far from where the capture occurred, the life of an eighty-eight-year old man came to a peaceful end and his name drifted into obscurity.

The name of that man, Cadwallader Colden, brings into focus an individual who served the Colony of New York for over a half century, longer by far than any of his contemporaries. Throughout that period, he remained unwaveringly devoted to the British monarchy. As such, he became one of the most reviled New York colonial figures. His name also identifies a physician, scientist, botanist, ethnographer, and philosopher; a savant, who was deemed

9

by colonial intellectuals as the most knowledgeable individual in all of the land. He shared an interest and dialogue with three other colonial physicians, who were similarly notable for diverse contributions beyond the realm of medicine.

Colden generated a large corpus of correspondence with the most notable scientists and thoughtful men, both in America and on the other side of the Atlantic Ocean. This is evidenced by a nine-volume publication by the New York Historical Society containing his correspondence. Yet, with all his recognized accomplishments and contemporary visibility, the name of Cadwallader Colden does not appear in the famous *Autobiography of Benjamin Franklin*, with whom Colden was engaged in an extensive correspondence. Their letters speak to a mutual high regard. Nor has Colden's long, productive, and influential life been the subject of a published biography, with the exception of a rarely read 1906 doctoral thesis[1] and a recent addition to *Contributions in American History*.[2] Both of these works essentially compartmentalize Cadwallader Colden's intellectual pursuits.

What has been lacking is a historical correlation between Cadwallader Colden's personal and political life with his many and varied intellectual pursuits. As a husband and father, he maintained constant concern for his large family, whose members reciprocated with admiration and strong emotional ties. The results are apparent in a consideration of the family's genealogy. His positive and praiseworthy familial relationships contrasted with his public persona, which was characterized by the inability to relate to political associates. Compromise and compassion were absent from his political lexicon.

His dedication to intellectual enquiry was unique for his position and location, but it was tainted by a desperate need for recognition and accolade. He was devoid of an appreciation of his intellectual capabilities, consequent to the absence of a firm basis in mathematics. Although he gained respect, it was never sufficient. The name of Cadwallader Colden, which could have become a beacon in the colonies and persisted for ages, has been diminished and erased with time. The sequence of life for arguably the most notable New York colonist was famed, flawed, forgotten!

CHAPTER 1

ꞔꞔ *Chapter 1* ꞔꞔ

BEFORE TAKING ROOT

1688–1718

*C*ounter to the usual course in which the Scotch-Irish immigrants to colonial America joined in with rebellious factions, Cadwallader Colden (fig. 1) never diverted from his dedication to British rule and his obligation to the Crown. This can be ascribed, in part, to his genetic and acquired conservatism related to the early parental influence during his youth. Colden was born in Ireland on February 7, 1688,[a] to Scottish parents, the Reverend Alexander Colden and his wife, Janet Hughes. Alexander Colden had received an MA from the University of Edinburgh in 1675, and, in 1685, he was ordained as a Presbyterian minister. He was initially assigned to a parish in Enniscorty, County Wexford, Ireland, where Cadwallader was born. A year after Cadwallader's birth, his father was transferred to the Presbytery of Duns, Scotland, about thirty miles from Edinburgh. His parents would remain at that post for the rest of their lives.[1]

In Alexander Colden's final letter to his son,[2] dated August 5, 1732, in which it is noted that Cadwallader's mother died on September 23, 1731, Cadwallader's father proudly reported that, at the time, he had the distinction of being the oldest minister in the Church of Scotland. In that letter, as in all of his correspondence, Cadwallader Colden's father's rigid religiosity is evident. The narrative of each letter assumed a ministerial tone as the pen

Figure 1. Cadwallader Colden. Portrait of Cadwallader Colden by John Wollaston (The Younger), 1749–1752. Oil on Canvas. Courtesy of the Metropolitan Museum of Art, bequest of Grace Wilkes, 1922 (22.45.6). All rights reserved, the Metropolitan Museum of Art.

issued forth pages of sermonizing directed at his son. It was as if the son was a member of the father's congregation.

Cadwallader's youth was spent in a bucolic environment, not far from the east coast of southern Scotland. As a young teenager, he was sent to the University of Edinburgh in preparation for following in his father's ministerial footsteps. Cadwallader was admitted in 1702 and matriculated in February 1703, entering as a second-year student because of his proficiency in Latin and Greek.[3]

As part of his studies, Cadwallader was exposed to botany, which was an integral part of the curriculum. The subject had been added to the roster of courses at the University of Edinburgh in 1676. At that time, it was stated: "[C]onsidering the usefulness and necessity of encouragement of the art of Botany and planting of medicinal herbs, and that it were for the better flourishing of the College that the said profession be joined to the other professions, they appoint Mr. James Sutherland, present Botanist, who professes the said art; and upon consideration aforesaid, they unite, annex, and adjoin the said Profession to the rest of the liberal sciences taught in the College, and recommend the Treasurer of the College to provide a convenient room in the College for keeping books and seeds relative to the said Profession."[4] The subject, in which Cadwallader would maintain a long-term interest, was introduced to him by Dr. Charles Preston, the author of *Hortus Medicus Edinburgensis*.[5]

Colden graduated with an MA from the University of Edinburgh in 1705. Stimulated by his study of the sciences, including Newtonian science and general physics, Cadwallader forsook his father's plan and elected to study medicine in London, where, within a period of five years, he completed a course in anatomy with Doctor Ariskine and a course in chemistry with Mr. Wilson, both distinguished in their professions.[6] As Colden later confessed in a letter to the Swedish botanist Peter Kalm, he was unable to establish a medical practice that would sustain him in London, and so in 1710, he accepted the invitation of Mrs. Elizabeth Hill, his mother's widowed and childless sister, to join her in Philadelphia, at the time, a community with less than three thousand inhabitants. There, he planned to pursue his medical career while assisting his aunt in her mercantile business.[7]

The business, which concentrated on trade with the West Indies, took Colden to Barbados, Jamaica, Antigua, and St. Kitts. The bills of lading of the trade chronicled shipments of the two-way traffic that was dominated by sailings between Philadelphia, the busiest colonial port at the time, and, mainly, Barbados, the largest of the British colonies in the Caribbean Sea. Sugar, rum, and molasses were shipped from the islands, while bread, flour, meat, dry goods, and Madeira wine were sent from North America to the West Indies. One consignment from Colden in Philadelphia includes a "Negro Woeman & Child." She was described as "a good House Negro understands the work of the Kitchen perfectly & washes well. She has a natural aversion to all strong Liquors. Were it not for her Allusive Tongue her sullenness & the Custome of the Country that will not allow us to use our Negroes as you doe in Barbados when they Displeas you I would not have parted with her."[8]

In 1715, Colden interrupted his work in Philadelphia and traveled to Great Britain, where, that year, he married Alice Chrystie (fig. 2), the daughter of a Scottish minister in Kelso, about twenty miles from where he had spent his own youth. Alice was two years Cadwallader's junior and the sister of his friend and classmate at Edinburgh. Colden and his wife would eventually parent ten children, eight of whom would survive infancy. Colden's visit home coincided with the First Scottish Rebellion, known as "The Fifteen," in which there was an attempt to return the Stuarts to the throne. In a subsequent letter, written in support of Colden, in order to counter the criticism that he was a Jacobite rather than a staunch unionist, it was pointed out that, "on the News of McIntoshes

Figure 2. Alice Christy Colden. Portrait of Alice Christy Colden by John Wollaston (The Younger), 1749-1752. Oil on Canvas. Courtesy of the Metropolitan Museum of Art, bequest of Grace Wilkes, 1922 (22.45.6). All rights reserved, the Metropolitan Museum of Art.

Landing on the South Side of the First of Edinburgh he [Colden] brought upward of Seventy Men from the Parish where his Father lives and continued with your Lordship [the Marquis of Lothian] under Arms at Kelso several days."[9]

During that 1715 trip, which was the last time Colden returned home, he met Edmund Halley, the famous astronomer whose name was attached to the comet, the orbit of which he had defined. Colden visited the Royal Society, which received and published his first scientific paper, "Animal Secretions."[10]

The married couple arrived back in Philadelphia in 1716. On his return, Colden concentrated to a greater extent on his medical career. He purchased a barometer and thermometer, from Edinburgh and sent for "any thing that is new in Medicine Mathematics History or Poetry, including the last edition of *Newton's Optics* and Dr. Gregory's astronomical tables."[11] Among the medical texts ordered by Colden were: *Le Clerc Histoire de la Medicine, Hovius de Circulari Humoum, Motie in Oculis, Nuck Operationes et Experiment Chirurg, Wepfer Historia Cicutae Acquaticae, Banister Herbarium Vorgineanum, Artis Medice Principles published by Borheowe, Ruyschs Observation.*[12] He also ordered a variety of drugs from an apothecary in addition to mortars, crucibles, and Glyster pipes.[13]

Colden, as a formally trained physician, was a member of a distinct minority. William Smith, Jr., in the first volume of *The History of the Province of New-York*, covering a time period that ended in 1732, wrote: "Quacks abound like Locusts in *Egypt*, and too many have recommended themselves to a full Practice and a profitable Subsistence. This is the less to be wondered at, as the Profession is under no Kind of Regulation. Loud as the call is, to our Shame be it remembered, we have no Law to protect the Lives of the King's Subjects, from the Malpractice of Pretenders. Any Man at his Pleasure sets up for Physician, Apothecary, and Chirurgeon. No Candidates are either examined or licensed, or even sworn to fair Practice."[14]

Only one of Boston's ten practitioners had a foreign medical degree in 1720, and only one of nine Virginia physicians of the eighteenth century had attended medical school.[15] William Douglass, the one Boston physician with a foreign medical degree, in the 1750s wrote: "by living a year or two in any quality with a practitioner of any sort, apothecary, cancer doctor, cutter for stone, bone-setters, tooth-drawer, &c. with the essential fundamentals of ignorance and impudence, is esteemed to qualify himself for all the branches of the medical art, as much or more than gentlemen in Europe well born, liberally educated (and therefore modest likewise) [who] have travelled much, attended medical professors of many denominations, frequented city hospitals, and camp, infirmaries, &c. for many years."[16] At the time of the American Revolution only 5 percent of medical practitioners held a recognized medical degree.[17]

An eighteenth-century Virginia practitioner, who had trained under the apprenticeship system, countered that "those self swollen sons of pedantic absurdity, fresh & raw from that universal asylum of medical perfection, Edinburgh, . . . [who] enter with obstinate assurance upon the old round of obsolete prescription, which their infallible masters taught them, &, like the mule that turns aside for no man, push on in their bloody career till the surrounding mortality, but more especially the danger of their own thick skulls, brings them to pause, & works in them a new conviction."[18]

Colden is credited with the first attempt to establish a systematic course of medical lectures in the colonies.[19] He directed his proposal to James Logan, an influential Philadelphia politician with an interest in science, including botany and Newtonian physics, who was the cousin of Colden's wife. Logan was described as "the region's most influential statesman, its most distinguished scholar, its respected—though not its most beloved—citizen.[20] Logan had invited Colden to assist him in using a telescope to observe an eclipse of the sun in order to compare observations made by astronomers in England. As is noted in a letter by James Logan, written May 1, 1717, in addition to Colden's educational proposal, he requested that an arrangement be established in which he could be compensated for taking care of the poor.

He [Colden] came to me one day to desire my opinion of a proposal to get an act of Assembly for an allowance for him as physician for the poor of this place. I told him I thought very well of the thing, but doubted whether it could be brought to bear in the House. Not long after R. Hill showed me a bill for this purpose, put in his hands by the Governor, with two further provisions in it, which were, that a public physical lecture should be held in Philadelphia, to the support of which every unmarried man above twenty-one years, should pay six shillings, eight-pence, or an English crown yearly, and that the corpses of all persons that died here should be visited by an appointed physician, who should receive for his trouble three shillings and four-pence. These things I owned very commendable, but doubted our Assembly would never go into them, that of lectures especially.[21]

In 1718, Colden's life changed rapidly and dramatically. The change would provide for him the platform for his political performance and the opportunity to satisfy his intellectual curiosity. It began when Colden casually visited New York and, in accordance with protocol, called upon the governor of the province, Robert Hunter. Hunter was a fellow Scot, who had apprenticed to an apothecary but ran away and joined the army. He rose in the ranks, married a woman of high status, and served under the Duke of Marlborough until 1709 when he was made governor of New York. Hunter was an intellect, a classical scholar, linguist, poet, amateur scientist, and a member of the Royal Society of London. Hunter was immediately impressed with Colden's potential as an aide in the governance of the province of New York.

Hunter sought an endorsement for Colden and, in response to Colden's request for a recommendation to Hunter, Logan wrote that it was, "too much like a man's desiring his wife to speak on behalf of another woman. . . . My heart goes against my head" and if "Colden were doomed to leave Philadelphia, I should wish him at New York, and can say no further."[22] About two weeks after Colden's visit to New York, he received a letter from Governor Hunter offering him the position of surveyor general and master in chancery. Colden immediately accepted and moved with his family to New York.

↔ *Chapter 2* ↔
A NEW NEW YORKER
1718–1728

*T*he stage on which Cadwallader Colden developed and augmented the recognition, respect, and notability that he enjoyed during his lifetime, was a relatively recent consequence of the efforts of European and English powers to expand their influence in the Western Hemisphere. At the time that Colden moved from Philadelphia to the Province of New York, where he would serve that colony for the remaining fifty-eight years of his life, New York had been a British possession for fifty-two years, less one brief interruption. New York was but one of a series of British acquisitions and developments, having been preceded by several royal colonies and proprietary grants and to be followed by others.

The English attempt at settlement on the North American continent was initiated in 1578 when Sir Humphrey Gilbert received from Queen Elizabeth I letters of patent to search for land in North America. In 1583, Gilbert set out across the Atlantic Ocean to establish the settlement but his ship sank in a storm. His royal grant was transferred to his half-brother, Walter Raleigh, who in 1584 sent Captain Philip Amadas and the gentleman Arthur Barlowe to search for an appropriate site for a colony in North America. They came upon an island known to the Native Americans as "Roanoke," and, on their return to England, they issued reports encouraging colonization as a means of dealing with their surplus population.

Sir Walter Raleigh, who had been recently knighted, received the royal allowance to establish a permanent colony in the area. This was to serve as a base for further exploration and as a supply depot for ships to privateer against the Spanish fleet. Raleigh also received permission to name that colony "Virginia" honoring Elizabeth I, the "virgin queen." With Raleigh's sponsorship, in 1585, Sir Richard Grenville led a flotilla of seven ships and explored the Carolina sounds. He left Ralph Lane at Roanoke with 108 colonists to settle the region. The colony failed as a result of internal dissension and hostility of the local natives. In 1586, the colonists returned to England with Sir Francis Drake, who had completed an expedition of plundering the West Indies. Later that year, Grenville returned to the area and, finding the colony deserted, left a group of fifteen men as a holding force. They all perished and came to be known as the "Lost Colony." A year later, Raleigh dispatched 110 settlers under the leadership of John White to establish the "Cittie of Raleigh in Virginea," with specific instructions to locate the shore of Chesapeake Bay. However, they formed the settlement at Roanoke and it was there that Virginia Dare became the first English child to be born in the Western Hemisphere. John White sailed to England for supplies and, on his return to Roanoke in 1690, he noted that nothing was left of the second "Lost Colony."[1]

The first successful English settlement on the North American continent took place in the first decade of the seventeenth century after Queen Elizabeth had died and was succeeded by James I. A permanent settlement was established at Jamestown in 1607 and spread from that area with sufficient success to result in a large expanse of regional land to be designated the royal colony of Virginia in 1624.

After the colonization of Plymouth in 1620, the next royal

charter, designated as the Massachusetts Bay Colony, was granted in 1629 by Charles I, and settlement of the region broadened. Later, when Charles II was brought to the throne in 1660 during the English Restoration, the governmental policy became more focused on extending the Crown's influence over the colonies. Persistent resistance on the part of the colonists eventually led to the revocation of Massachusetts's charter and the establishment of the Dominion of New England by James II in 1684. After James II was deposed in 1688, the Massachusetts Colony was returned to rule under its original charter. Four years later, in 1692, a new charter was established for the Province of Massachusetts that incorporated the Plymouth Colony, Nantucket, and Martha's Vineyard.

Continuing the chronologic sequence of English colonization of North America, Maryland can be traced to 1632 when Charles I granted land to George Calvert, Lord Baltimore. The first settlers arrived two years later. In 1681, William and Mary made it a crown colony, but it reverted to its proprietary status in 1721. Connecticut began, in 1636, with the Old Saybrook Colony at the mouth of the river, which took its name from the Native American designation. That same year, the three up-river towns of Windsor, Wethersfield, and Hartford joined to establish the Connecticut Colony. In 1639, the New Haven Colony was formed. In 1666, the three colonies, Old Saybrook, Connecticut, and New Haven united under the title of Connecticut, but New Haven maintained a separate government until after the American Revolution.

Rhode Island and Providence Plantations was chartered as a Provincial entity in 1644. In 1686, it was added to the Dominion of New England. As was the case for Massachusetts, when the Dominion was disassembled, Rhode Island and Providence Plantations received its own royal charter in 1688. Carolina can trace its origin to the royal charter that eight Lords Proprietors received from Charles II in 1663. The encompassed land was given its name, the adjective for Charles, to honor the king. The area was divided into two distinct entities, North Carolina and South Carolina in 1712, but continued to be ruled by the Lords Proprietors until they became royal colonies in 1729.

Shortly after the Dutch surrendered New York to the English in 1664, Charles II assigned a large proprietary to his brother, the Duke of York. A portion of that land, which came to be known as New Jersey, was granted to Lord John Berkeley and George Carteret. There were initially two Jerseys, an East Jersey and a West Jersey. Both were annexed to the Dominion of New England from 1686 to 1688. In 1702, the proprietors returned the land to King George II, and it became a royal province under the governance of New York's governor.

New Hampshire was an independent royal province from 1679 to 1698 when it was placed under the jurisdiction of Massachusetts and that colony's governor until 1741. At that time, it returned to its original status as an individual colony with its own magistrate.

In 1681, as repayment for a long standing loan, a large land grant was made to William Penn. It was the genesis of Pennsylvania and included the Three Lower Counties (New Castle, Kent, and Sussex). The Three Lower Counties became the independent colony of Delaware in 1701, but, although there was a separate assembly, it was responsible to the governor of Pennsylvania. Georgia, the last of the original thirteen colonies to be settled, began in 1732 and became a crown colony in 1755.

Bringing into focus Cadwallader Colden's adopted colony of New York and a more expansive consideration of that colony with which he is indentified, there is a coincidental relation between the time of his birth in 1688 and the evolution of the colony. New York was unique among English colonies in the Western Hemisphere in that it had been settled initially by other than Englishmen, namely the Dutch. The final two years of the penultimate decade of the seventeenth century were transitional in the anglicization of the colony.

The English claim to possession of New York is evidenced in

a March 1664 charter by which Charles II granted his brother James, Duke of York, proprietary rights to a broad expanse of land. Included were Manhattan, the Hudson River, all of the land from the west side of the Connecticut River to the east side of Delaware Bay, all of Long Island, Nantucket, Martha's Vineyard, and parts of Maine. James, invoking his role as Lord High Admiral of England, immediately ordered a fleet under the command of Richard Nicolls to take possession of the granted lands. On September 8, 1664, the Dutch, led by Peter Stuyvesant, surrendered all the land within their settlement that they had named New Netherlands.

Although their power in the Western Hemisphere was in decline after the mid-point of the seventeenth century, the Dutch made an ultimate attempt to regain some control in 1673. The Dutch fleet laid siege to the defenseless island of Manhattan. On July 30, the English capitulated and the Dutch flag was raised. This was memorialized by a new issue of a classic map, showing a revised view of lower Manhattan. New Netherlands enjoyed a brief restoration that lasted until October 1674 when the region was relinquished to the English without a battle.

In 1667, the western half of Connecticut was returned to the eastern half, and the land along the western shore of the Delaware River was released to Lord Baltimore. Colonel Nicolls was assigned the responsibility for establishing laws and governing over the remaining land. Those laws initially applied only to the residents of Long Island and Westchester and had little influence on the Dutch settlers in Manhattan. Colonel Francis Lovelace succeeded Nicolls in 1668 and served in the capacity of governor for five years. During his tenure, Lovelace granted Martha's Vineyard, Nantucket, other small islands, and several manors that had been included in the Duke of York's domain to the duke's favorites.

In 1685, James II succeeded Charles II as king of England and Scotland, and the proprietary of New York became a royal colony. As such, it was deemed inappropriate to grant New Yorkers rights that exceeded those that had been given to settlers within the previously established American colonies. Therefore the New York Assembly, which had been constituted in 1683, was dissolved. Albany was granted a charter as a municipality in 1686 following the format that had been used for the municipality of New York three years previously. In 1688, the year of Colden's birth, in keeping with the other northern colonies, New York (including New Jersey) was incorporated in the Dominion of New England. In 1689, James II was deposed and William and Mary ascended the throne. Two years later, the original New York charter was renewed and persisted until after the American Revolution.

George I became king of Great Britain in 1716 and would rule until 1727. It was during his reign that Cadwallader Colden moved to New York City. The 1723 census for the colony reported approximately 19,000 white adults and 4,000 black adults.[2] New York City had about 7,000 white adults, most living south of current Wall Street. Colden, his wife, and son, Alexander, who was born in Philadelphia on August 13, 1716,[3] moved to the city of New York in the latter half of 1718.

The earliest date that can be affixed to the Coldens' residence in New York is October 6, 1718, on which day Colden petitioned for a grant of two thousand acres of land in Ulster County. The patent for the specified acreage, the largest parcel permitted for an individual, was issued to him on April 9, 1719.[4] Governor Hunter designated Colden Master of the Board of Chancery, a position in the judicial system of the colony of New York that had been established in 1701 and would persist as the court with jurisdiction on cases of equity until 1847. The most enticing aspect of Governor Hunter's recruitment of Colden was the prospect of becoming the surveyor general of New York. In the interim before that appointment could be finalized, Colden was appointed weigh-master of the Port of New York, ranger of Ulster and Orange Counties, in addition to master of the Board of Chancery.

In 1719, Hunter sailed for England on a leave of absence with the anticipation of returning, but the English leadership decided that he should exchange positions with William Burnet, who was comptroller of customs. During the period of Hunter's absence and awaiting the arrival of the newly appointed Governor Burnet, administration of the colony of New York was assumed by Colonel Peter Schuyler, who was the most senior member of the Council. Shortly thereafter, the surveyor general of New York, Augustine Graham, died, and Schuyler, who had been allied with individuals in opposition to Governor Hunter, appointed Captain Allane Jarratt to the position that had been promised to Cadwallader Colden. The unanticipated appointment was rapidly overturned by Colden's friends in court in London, and, in April 1720, Colden was formally designated surveyor general.[5] Colden, ultimately, was relieved of his anxiety when he was informed of his status in a letter from London, written on February 18, 1720, prior to a new governor's arrival In New York.[6]

Cadwallader Colden's personality as a politician became manifest early in regard to his attitude toward those whom he considered to be antagonists. He would often insert the failings of his foes into his political arguments, and neither forgave nor forgot over the course of time. Early in his official status as surveyor general, Colden indicated that the administration of the Land Office while Peter Schuyler directed the government was characterized by cheating and preferential consideration of the claims of political allies.[7] In a letter written to his son, Alexander, in 1760, recalling events forty years past, Colden declared that, in the absence of Governor Hunter, Schuyler retained all of the governor's salary rather than maintain half to be given to the governor on his return. Schuyler was characterized as "a weak man" in Colden's correspondence. The reason for Schuyler's removal from the Council, given by Colden, was "by proof of Col. Schuylers having committed the custody of the Kings seal to Mr. Philipse &

of Mr. Philpse's having received it into his custody. This was highly criminal. . . ."[7]

Colden would spend a pleasing first decade of service to the colony under the leadership of Governor Burnet, who was designated governor of New York and New Jersey and would move on to become governor of Massachusetts in 1728. Governor William Burnet arrived in New York in September 1720. He was the son of the Bishop of Salisbury and the godson of William, Prince of Orange, later William III of England. In the determination and execution of policy, Burnet relied mainly on Chief Justice Lewis Morris, Cadwallader Colden, and James Alexander. Colden enjoyed the status of a favorite son. In 1721, Colonel Peter Schuyler and his confidant Adolph Philipse, members of the opposition, were removed from the Board of Council and replaced by Colden and Alexander.[8]

The Council consisted of twelve members who were appointed by the governor and served in an advisory fashion at his will. Next to the governor its members enjoyed the highest social prestige. The office of the president of the Council was usually reserved for the eldest member, although exceptions occurred during Colden's tenure of over five decades.

During Burnet's tenure as governor of New York, Colden's first decade in the colony concentrated on his activities as surveyor general, on Indian affairs, and on his role in the upper echelon of Burnet's administration. He divorced himself from the practice of medicine, but maintained a lifelong interest in the field. In 1720, he authored "An Account of the Diseases and Climate of New York."[9] Colden's continued interest in medicine is evidenced by several subsequent publications and his continuous correspondence with medical colleagues. Shortly after his move to New York, Colden summarized his concern regarding the practice of colonial medicine to Governor Hunter: "I doubt if these Incumbrances which hinder the Improvement of Medicine can be remov'd without the Assistance of our Rulers and Governors who dispense Rewards and Punishments and this has encouraged me to this Subject to write your Excellency on it."[10] Colden went on to explain the low repute of medicine: "The Hopes of sordid Gain has made Men ignorant of all the Sciences of Obscure and of no education intrude themselves. . . . By whose means the Art is become in many places Contemptible and curious learned men have been deterr'd from inquiring into this Science looking upon it as a Jungle of Hard Words without certain Foundation."[11]

Medicine was a common ground for many of the intellectual colonists with whom Colden related and established long-term correspondences. William Douglass, John Mitchell, and Alexander Garden shared their thoughts with Colden about medical subjects and, like Colden, maintained a profound interest in botany, physics, and philosophical thinking.

WILLIAM DOUGLASS

William Douglass, the first physician to be included in Colden's extensive correspondence, was known to Colden for the longest period of time. Douglass was about three years younger than Colden and was born in Gifford, Scotland, less than twenty miles from Colden's home. He studied at Edinburgh at the same time as Colden but received his MD from Utrecht in 1712. Douglass first arrived in Boston in 1716, and, after an interlude of two years in the West Indies, he returned to Boston, where he would spend the remainder of his life as the only physician in that city with a medical degree. The first letter from Douglass to Colden that appears in the Colden Papers is dated February 20, 17[20/21a]. After offering a profile of the practice of medicine in Boston in response to a letter from Colden, Douglass focused on an extensive history of the winds and weather in Boston for the previous year. Douglass mentioned his collection of over seven hundred plants within five miles of Boston—evidence of a broad interest in botany on the part of the colonial American intelligentsia.[12]

Subsequent letters from Douglass to Colden during that decade describe a smallpox epidemic in Boston in 1721,[13] astronomical issues,[14] their common interest in making a correct map of North America,[15] the description of an earthquake that took place in New England in 1727,[16] the political situation in Massachusetts,[17] and Douglass's condemnation of the use of paper money.[18] Douglass, like Colden, initially opposed Cotton Mather's enthusiasm for inoculation, but he later recanted and administered inoculations himself.[19] Contained within Colden's letters to Douglass during that decade, in an undated letter probably written in 1728, Colden presented his proposal for the establishment of the first learned society in America.

I wish that a certain number of Men would enter into a Voluntary Society for the advancing of Knowledge & that for this purpose such in ye Neighbouring provinces as are most likely to be willing to promote this design be invited to enter it That the Society be confin'd to a certain Number in each Province And because the greatest number of proper persons are likely to be found in your Colony that the Members residing in or near Boston have the chief Direction That every member oblige himself to furnish a paper at least once in every six months on such subject as he shall best like for ye advancing our knowledge in any of the Arts or Sciences Which paper shall be transmitted to a Secretary to be chosen for that purpose who shall communicate it to the Members residing in or near Boston & they having examined it shall by ye Secretary signify to ye Author what objections they have to and part of it who thereupon may if he pleases correct what he thinks upon their observation deserves Correction & then the paper to be published for ye Benefit of the Absent Members & all others that shall desire to be inform'd in such matters It may be hoped that these papers by their Sale may be some recompence to the Secretary for his trouble & the necessary Expenses of the

Society The Gov[r] may find ways to lessen the Charge of Postage I
can only give some general Hints which I hope you will improve
& I shall think my self very lucky if you think them so well started
that they deserve pursuing The Rules for this Society must be
form'd at Boston & afterwards communicated to those you think
fit to invite into it [20]

In a letter dated February 17, 17[35/36], Douglass informed
Colden of the formation in Boston of the colonies' first medical
society.[21] In November 1739, Douglass wrote to Colden describing
an epidemic characterized by a "malignant Fever that was probably
Diphtheria.[22] Douglass died on October 21, 1752. His book, which
was published posthumously in 1755, entitled *A Summary, Historical
and Political of the First Planting, Progressive Improvements, and Present
State of the British Settlements in North America*, includes a map, *Plan
of British Dominions of New England*. This very rare, seminal map
was the basis for the popular "Map of the Most Inhabited Part of
New England" published two years later in London by Thomas
Jefferys.[23]

* * *

Colden's initial energies as a servant of the province of New York
were consumed by his role as surveyor general. In the beginning
of 1720, he found the affairs of the office that he had assumed to
be in total confusion and disarray. This was inevitable because of
the policies, which had been employed for granting land while
New York was a proprietary of the Duke of York and throughout
its slightly over a half century as a royal colony. From the onset in
the proprietary, when the grants were generally in the range of
two hundred acres or less, surveys were not performed and the
boundaries were ill-defined. Similarly, the rents were imprecise
and bore no relationship to the quantity or quality of the land.

After New York became a royal province and the governors

were empowered to grant lands, although it was specified that the grants were to be surveyed by the public surveyor and recorded with the seal of New York, compliance was uncommon.[24] From the time of the first royal governor, Thomas Dongan, when there were no true surveys but rather descriptions and estimates, lack of adherence to the stated rules persisted. Boundaries were frequently described as bounded by a certain Indian's land, disregarding the fact that the Indians were never truly landowners in an individual capacity.[25]

The governor of New York between 1701 and 1708, Edward Hyde, Lord Cornbury, who was characterized by historians as a "degenerate and pervert who is said to have spent half of his time dressed in women's clothes,"[26] added to the problem of land ownership that was encountered by Colden. To one group, Lord Cornbury granted the Indian tract Wawayanda, in Orange County, with unnamed borders, and, to another group, the Great Minnisink patent in Delaware County. In that instance, the boundary was described as beginning at "the Indian hunting-house" when there were several hundred such houses in that vicinity.[27]

On taking office, Colden was urged by Chief Justice Lewis Morris to delay grants to members of the opposition until Governor Burnet arrives. Morris wrote:

[A]ll the power Either they or you have in the disposition of lands is deriv'd from the king who has been pleas'd to direct that your consent be had to any land granted which consent you will not give unless the land be first Set out by you in which allocation you will allwaies Endeavor to follow the kings royall Instructions in that behalf given; that you will at all times be very ready to returne any tract of land pursuant to the directions of that hon[ble] board or give A consent to Any Grant when you are well Assured the So doing will not be A breach of duty & the trust his majestie has been pleas'd to repose in you. As for Bud the case is a little ticklish he being of the assembly may be prejudiciall to you in your office and another difficulty is he being chose by the Interest of a party that won't breake their hearts should the governour not returne & the revenue being to Settle if he should be serv'd during this administration it will make him less dependent on the Governour than he should be, for the hopes of favours will make many in that house more tractable than the Strongest reasons offr'd wthout the case is the Same wth some others. . . .[28]

Colden's first surveys were conducted in the sparsely settled Orange and Ulster Counties. In 1694, it was the area in which Captain John Evans had received a grant that was sealed by the Colonial Assembly of New York in 1698 and approved by Queen Anne in 1709.[29] By the end of his first year in office, Colden had surveyed 18,960 acres of that patent and 14,516 acres in the adjacent region.[30] From that original patent, shortly after arriving in New York, Colden obtained a grant of 3,000 acres (an initial patent for 2,000 acres followed by an additional grant of 1,000 adjacent acres), on which he later built his farm, which he named "Coldengham," a variation of Coldingham, Berwickshire, Scotland, which was located five miles from the home of his youth. Coldengham subsequently became part of the town of Montgomery in Orange County.

During his first seven years as surveyor general, Colden spent much of his time in the Mohawk Valley; the Shawangunk Mountains reaching from the area around Newburgh, New York, to the New Jersey border; the Catskill Mountains; the region around Albany, Orange, and Ulster Counties; and the Westchester estates and the Connecticut border. As evidence of Colden's strict adherence to the letter of the law, Colden's office certified or issued no grants without a proper survey. In his capacity as surveyor general, in the spring of 1725, Colden was one of the three representatives of New York to meet with the commissioners and surveyor from Connecticut for the first time to define a contested boundary between the two colonies.

In the course of surveying the Mohawk Valley, Colden gained an appreciation of the Five Nations of Indians that made up the Iroquois. In September 1721, Colden accompanied Governor William Burnet to Albany for a conference with the Five Nations. Before the meeting, Burnet and Colden visited the small village of Schenectady and viewed the Cohoes Falls on the Mohawk River. The meeting took place at the Indians' Lodge house. About eighty sachems (Indian chieftains) were present and the governor expressed concern over the recently built French trading post at Niagara. The Indians were encouraged to trade with the British at Albany and avoid trading with the French. At the conclusion of the meeting, the Iroquois promised to cease further trading with the French and to provide free passage to all Indians trading with Albany. In his report, Colden commented on the appearance and social structure of the Five Nations and emphasized that "their Cruelty in my opinion sullys any good quality which they may have especially to their enemys which they over come." He made reference to torture and cannibalism.[31]

Colden's association with the Five Nations formed the basis for two significant contributions, one to the cartography of North America and the other to colonial descriptive literature. In 1721, William Bradford, New York's first resident printer, published Cadwallader Colden's "A MAP of the Countrey of THE FIVE NATIONS belonging to the province of NEW-YORK and of the LAKES near which the Nations of FAR INDIANS live with part of CANADA taken from the Map of LOUISIANE done by Mr DeLisle in 1718" (fig. 3). This rare map is considered to be the first map published in the province. The map was first published separately and subsequently appeared in 1724 in Colden's *Papers Relating to an Act of New-York for Encouragement of the Indian Trade*, which was also printed by William Bradford.[32]

It is a relatively crude map, which is almost a precise magnification of the map that appears as a frontispiece in Baron La Hontan's

1702 book.[33] Colden's map, however, contains added details related to the Five Nations. It depicts an area extending from the southern portion of Canada to the middle of Maryland, from the Hudson River to the middle of Lake Michigan. It locates each of the Five Nations (Mohawks, Oneidas, Onondagas, Cayugas, and Senecas), and the lands to the west conquered by the Five Nations. It depicts several "carrying places" of portage. In an included script, it is noted that the Tuscaroras had joined the Iroquois as a sixth nation in 1723. The "Map of LOUISIANE," from which Colden indicated that his map was taken, is a landmark in the cartography of North America. This large, expansive, and detailed

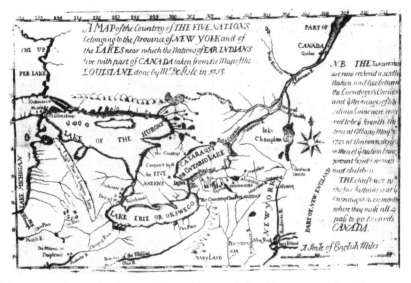

Figure 3. Cadwallader Colden, "A Map of the Countrey of the Five Nations belonging to the province of New York and of the Lakes near which the Nations of Far Indians live with part of Canada taken from the Map of the Louisiane done by Mr DeLisle in 1718." Engraving 23 x 37 cm. Printed by William Bradford, New York. Published separately and also appeared in Colden's Papers Relating to an Act of New York for Encouragement of the Indian Trade (New York, 1724). Courtesy of Private Collector.

map by Guillaume Delisle, the leading French mapmaker at the time of publication in 1718, is regarded as the main source for all later maps of the Mississippi River and the first large-scale map to accurately show the lower Mississippi and surrounding area. It is also the first map to contain the name Texas (Mission de Teijas).[34]

Colden's interest in cartography persisted. He was unsuccessful in an attempt to obtain funding from the government for a map of the colony of New York based on his surveys and involvement in intercolonial boundary commissions. He later wrote this to Peter Collinson: "We have but too much reason to be sensible in the great Defects of Geography of North America not withstanding that in many cases it must be useful and in some necessary to our Ministers to have a true Account of our Coasts & most consider-able plans on it as well as our Merchants."[35]

Colden's significant contribution to colonial America's litera-ture, *The History of the Five Indian Nations*, was published by William Bradford in New York in 1727. The printing of five hundred copies quickly sold out to a colonial, English, and European audience.[36] It was critically acclaimed by the contemporary readership. In 1755, John Huske wrote: "As to the Histories of the Indians . . . not one [is] worth reading but that of Colden."[37] In 1757, William Smith, Jr., an outspoken critic of Cadwallader Colden, in *The History of the Province of New York*, relied a great deal upon Colden's work. Smith "found some passages accurate, some inaccurate and others incorrect, and noted carefully where Colden and Charlevoix, the French Jesuit contradicted each other."[38]

Colden's literary reputation was established by the publication of *The History of the Five Indian Nations* as evidenced by its imme-diate popularity and its subsequent expansion and publications. Lawrence C. Wroth, the librarian of the John Carter Brown Library and the Rosenbach Fellow in Bibliography, points out that the nar-rative is an important part of the corpus of colonial literature.[39] Colden indicated in the preface:

THOUGH every one that in the least acquainted with the Affairs of North-America, knows of what Consequence the Indians, commonly known to the people of New-York by the Name of the Five Nations, are both in Peace and War, I know of no Accounts of them Published in English, but what are meer Translations of French Authors. This seems to throw some Reflection on the Inhabitants of this Province, As if we wanted Curiosity to enquire into our own Affairs, and that we were willing to rest satisfied with the Accounts the French give us of our own Indians, notwithstanding that the French in Canada are always in a different Interest, and sometimes in open Hostility with us. This Consideration, I hope will justify my attempting to write an History of the Five Nations at this time; and my endeavoring to remove the Blame with which we may be charged, perhaps will atone for many Faults which the want of Capacity may have occasioned.

Having had the Perusal of the Minutes of the Commissioners for Indian Affairs, I have been enabled to collect many Materials for this History, which are not to be found any where else; And this Collection will, at least be useful to any Persons of more Capacity, who shall afterwards undertake this task. . . .[40]

Colden specifically credits the works of Mr. de Bacquevillle de la Potherie[41] and Mr. Baron de Lahontan.[42] The book is dedicated to Governor William Burnet and focuses on the favorable relationships between the Five Nations and the province of New York and other colonies and the attempts of the French in Canada to disrupt those relationships. Colden begins with a brief description of the government of the confederacy of the Five Nations, which the Tuscaroras had recently joined, and the structure of the Nations themselves. What follows are anecdotal descriptions of six segments of history that occurred in the seventeenth century and impacted on the Five Nations and their relationships with the English and French colonists. Despite Colden's extensive involvement with the Indians, however, the work incorporates none of his personal knowledge or any recent or contemporary issues.

Colden had a positive impression of the individual members of the Five Nations (Iroquois), and, despite an appreciation of their deficiencies and some patterns of behavior, he championed their cause. He wrote:

> The Five Nations are a poor Barbarous People, under the darkest Ignorance, and yet a bright and noble Genius shines thro' these black Clouds. None of the greatest Roman Heros have discovered a greater Love to their Country, or a greater Contempt of Death than these Barbarians have done, when Life and Liberty came in Competition: Indeed, I think our Indians have out-done the Romans in this particular; for some of the greatest Romans have Murder'd themselves to avoid Shame of Torments, (a) Whereas our Indians have refused to Dye meanly with the least pain, when they thought their Country's Honour would be at stake, by it, but gave their Bodies willingly up to the most cruel Torments of their Enemies, to shew, that the Five Nations consisted of Men whose Courage and Resolution could not be Shaken. The sully, however, those noble Vertues by that cruel Passion Revenge, which they think not only lawful, but Honourable to exert without Mercy on their Country's Enemies, and for this only they deserve the Name of Barbarians.
>
> But what have we Christians done to make them better? Alas! We have reason to be ashamed, that these Infidels, by our Conversation and Neighbourhood, are become worse than they were before they knew us. Instead of Vertues we have only taught them Vices, that they were entirely free of before that time. The narrow Views of private Interest have occasioned this, and will occasion greater, even Publick Mischiefs, if the Governors of the People do not, like true Patriots, exert themselves, and put a stop to these growing Evils, If these Practices be winked at, instead of faithful Friends that have Manfully fought our Battles for us, the Five Nations will becaome faithless Thieves and Bobbers, and joyn with every Enemy that can give them the hopes of Plunder,
>
> If care were taken to plant in them, and cultivate that General Benevolence of Mankind, which is the true Principle of Vertue, it would effectually eradicate those horrid Vices occasioned by Unbound Revenge; and then the Five Nations would no longer

deserve the name of Barbarians, but would become a People whose Friendship might add Honour to the British Nation tho' they be now too generally despised. [43]

Indicative of the confidence and esteem that the Indians held for Colden was his adoption by the Mohawks of Canajoharie.

During his first decade as a New Yorker, Cadwallader Colden's role of a colonial politician formally began with the arrival of Governor William Burnet in New York. In one of Burnet's first letters to Parliament, he suggested the appointment of Colden as Councilor and, at the same time, proposed James Alexander, a Scotsman and close friend of Colden, for a second position on the Council.[44] These had been vacated by the removal of Peter Schuyler and Adolph Philipse. Colden took his seat on the Council for the first time on May 30, 1722.[45]

In 1723, Colden prepared a comprehensive memorandum for London officials that detailed the state of commerce in colonial New York.[46] It is considered to be the most definitive description of the time. The memorandum emphasized the colony's dependence on foreign trade and the fact that wheat and flour were the major export commodities.[47] The report was an attempt to convince Great Britain that restrictive measures related to the commerce with her colonies would be counterproductive.

In 1724, Colden became a communicant of Trinity Church and he remained a devout Christian. But, he believed that the pleasures of life and pursuit of enjoyment through intellectual interests did not lessen the devotion to God.[48] "A Memorial concerning the Fur Trade of the Province of New York presented to His Excellency William Burnet, Esquire, Captain Generall & Governor &c By Cadwallader Colden, Surveyor General of said Province, November 10th, 1724" was printed for distribution. It was an expression of the governor's policy for trade with the Indians and a rebuttal of the criticisms of the merchants who opposed the policy. A small trading post had been built on the southern shore of Lake Ontario and the Indians were encouraged to use that post and also to trade with the English in Albany rather than the French in Canada. Direct trade between the English and French merchants was disallowed by the Import Act that was approved by the Board of Trade. Powerful merchants in New York and London, believing that their profits were being threatened, launched an attack on the governor's policy, and had the act repealed. In response, Colden's Memorial indicated that, in their argument to the Board of Trade, the merchants blatantly misrepresented the facts. They had erroneously stated that "*Besides the Nations of* Indians *that are in the* English *Interest, there are very many Nations of* Indians, *who are at present in the Interest of the* French, *and who lie between New-York.*"[49]

Colden's report was factual, but was nuanced by negative and polarized attacks on the New York merchants who had misrepresented the facts. Although specific names were not mentioned, Colden's expressed personal grievance against those in opposition was characteristic of his argumentative and unforgiving personality. Subsequently, Colden issued a scathing attack on George Clarke, a member of the Council and one of the largest land owners in the province and an influential politician. Clarke would become lieutenant governor of New York in 1737, at which time Colden and he reconciled their differences. Colden also incurred the lifelong antipathy of the influential Delancey family when he refused to qualify Stephen Delancey as a member of the Assembly because his citizenship was deemed doubtful. Colden, throughout his life, provoked critics—a factor that clouded his accomplishments and, in part, was responsible for an inappropriate lack of recognition of his contributions. Colden's report was a significant and influential factor, which led the Board of Trade to overturn the repeal and, thereby, approve the governor's policy related to the fur trade.

In the colony of New York during the 1720s conflicts over the relative merits of free trade, as contrasted with protective duties, were pervasive and dominated politics. In 1726, two pamphlets espousing the competing arguments were printed. *The Interest of the Country in laying Duties: or, a Discourse, shewing how Duties on some Sorts of Merchandize may make the Province of New-York richer than it would be without them* was written by Colden and printed as an anonymous document by John Peter Zenger. It was countered by another anonymous document, also printed by Zenger. *The Interest of City and Country to Lay No Duties: or A Short Discourse shewing that Duties on Trade, tend to the Impoverishing City and Country.* In response to the two disparate publications, Colden produced a pamphlet, also printed in 1726 by Zenger, *The Two Interests reconciled; occasioned by two late Pamphlets, called The Interest of the Country and the Interest of City and Country.* Disguised as an attempt at reconciliation, Colden's publication was a partisan expression that called for a direct tax upon land accumulators or usurers, a locally built and home-owned merchant marine, and a continuation of protective duties.[50]

In addition, there is a draft in Colden's handwriting, *The Second Part of the Interest of the Country in Laying Duties*, that is included in the publications of *The Letters and Papers of Cadwallader Colden*. He had an immutable suspicion and dislike of merchants and lawyers. In this document, Colden criticized the city merchants for their antagonism toward the payment of duties. He focused on the duties attached to the importation of liquor, indicating that if drinking would be reduced it would be advantageous for the country, ". . . & this further good may be expected that when strong Drink becomes dearer & a person more accustomed to work he may the sooner be reclaim'd & lose his ill habit."[51]

Also in 1726, Colden recorded a draft of a report of a Committee of Council concerning government revenues. It was written in response to a vote by the Assembly that put a restraint on the powers given to the governor to issue all monies. The Assembly indicated that its members ought to determine their compensation and have oversight of disposition of all the funds that the governor receives from the Crown. Colden's report affirmed that the control of "his Majesties Revenue" resides with the governor and the Council rather than the Assembly.[52]

Toward the end of Colden's period of residence in New York City, two letters that he received were dated April 2 and April 9, 1728, and were ascribed to Peter Collinson, who would remain an important correspondent with Colden for almost four decades. Peter Collinson was born in London on January 28, 1694, into a Quaker family that was engaged in the cloth trade, which he maintained, dealing in fabrics and haberdashery of every kind, until his retirement in 1765. Collinson developed an interest in botany, and received his first plants from North American soil in 1723. His lifelong interest in American plants served as a basis of continued correspondence with colonial Americans with similar interests, such as James Logan, John Bartram, John Clayton, Alexander Garden, and Cadwallader Colden. Collinson served as an intermediary between the American botanists and the English and European scientific world, particularly the botanists, Carolus Linnaeus and Johannes Fredericus Gronovius.[53]

The end of Colden's first decade in New York coincided with his move from the city to the country. Governor Burnet was transferred to the governorship of Massachusetts on April 15, 1728, and was replaced by Governor John Montgomerie, who would serve until his death in 1731. In a letter written on January 31, 1760, to his son, Alexander, Cadwallader Colden reflected on the impact that Montgomerie had on his personal status.

> As we were walking in formality to publish Colonel Montgomeries's commission, I overheard him say to Mr Clark that he would absolutely trust to his advice and he kept his promise to his death. . . .
> Colonel Montgomerie did not want natural abilities nor

any part of the education proper for a gentleman, but he had given himself up to his pleasures, especially to his bottle and had an aversion to business. He was likewise the most diffident of himself of any man I ever knew. He was much in debt and wanted to recover his fortune by the profits of his government with as little trouble to himself as possible. Mr. Clark served him well for these purposes.

Mr. DeLancey was at the head of the party in the assembly which had been in opposition to Mr. Burnet and which had now the ascendant in that house. Mr. DeLancey was to be gratified in his resentment against Chief Justice Morris and the Governor was to use his interest to have the acts repealed which had been passed in Governor Burnet's Administration prohibiting the direct trade to Canada with Indian goods. . . . Mr. DeLancey had the advantages of his own private trade in view which were very considerable.[54]

Coldengham is the residence with which Cadwallader Colden is generally identified. Work actually began on the farm in 1724 at which time Colden initially conceived of it as a vacation home. Before Colden began the development, the land "was the habitation only of wolves & bears & other wild animals."[55] Initially, the management of the farm was carried out by an overseer named Gallesby, but he was negligent of the care of the livestock and, consequently, fired.[56] Colden indicated in a letter to his aunt that he was building a small house and cellar under it. At the time, "My Design in this is that I may with some comfort be able three or four times a year to stay there a fortnight or three weeks & look after the Work that is done or what I may think proper."[57] According to the "Farm journal, 1727–1736, Coldengham, Orange County, N.Y.," a manuscript compiled by Colden, concentrated work began on the property during the summer of 1727.

Colden's Farm Journal, the manuscript of which is housed in the Rosenbach Museum and Library in Philadelphia, is the earliest extant New York farm journal for the Hudson Valley.[58]

The first entry bears the date April 15, 1727, and reads; "On the 15th of August we sow'd 4$^{1/16}$ Bushels Rye upon a summer fallow after Indian Corn. The ground was very mellow. Sow'd under furrow about 3 acres. At the same time sowed some spinage in the Garden." The journal chronicles crop rotation; planting of both white and yellow Indian corn; and establishing orchards of a variety of apples, cherries, pears, peaches, and nectarines. It also includes records of cattle breeding and butchering and dairying. A kitchen garden satisfied the culinary and medicinal needs.[59]

Coldengham, a 3,000-acre estate, is shown on a 1760 map to be located just to the west of the current Colden Cemetery at the corner where Tin Brook turns from east to north on the site of the Pimm House on Maple Avenue in Montgomery.[60] A deed dated September 7, 1771, by which Cadwallader Colden passed part of the property to his son, Cadwallader Colden, Jr., fixes the original Colden Mansion location as Maple Avenue just west of the cemetery in Montgomery.[61]

The move to Coldengham, where Colden would reside for the next three decades, was doubtless a consequence of his sensing a change in his potential for impact in the governing of New York. Colden maintained his role as councilor but moved with his family, which consisted of his wife and six young children (Alexander, born in Philadelphia August 13, 1716; Elizabeth, born in New York February 5, 1719; Cadwallader, born in New York May 26, 1722; Jane, born in New York March 27, 1724; Alice, born in New York September 27, 1725; and Sarah, born July 6, 1727). Mrs. Colden had also given birth to David between the births of Alexander and Elizabeth, but he died in infancy. The earliest specific date that can be ascribed to Colden's residence at Coldengham is November 19, 1728.[62]

The move was aimed at reducing his expenses, avoiding the frustrations generated by his political adversaries, and allowing leisure for philosophical study. In the letter that Colden had written to William Douglass in 1728, in which he suggested the for-

mation of a "Voluntary Society for the advancing of Knowledge,"
he stated:

> I hope I am now settled for some months free from the trouble-
> some broils which mens passions occasion in all publick affairs.
> This gives me hopes of being able to amuse myself with more
> innocent & more agreeable speculations than usually attend
> intrigues of State The speculations that gave you & me the
> greatest Pleasure in the pleasantest time of our Life while we
> were in the Garden of Eden before we knew good & Evil before
> we knew men. A Country life in many respects is very proper for
> these amusements while what is called nature in a strict sense
> is more open to our observation & while our thoughts are not
> drawn off by the unnatural pursuits of the busy part of mankind
> A man that has for sometime been tossed upon the Dunghill of
> mens Passions gratifies all his senses with the quiet & innocent
> pleasures that Nature freely offers in every step the he treds in
> the woods & fields. . . .[63]

Chapter 3
A COUNTRY GENTLEMAN REMAINS FOCUSED ON COLONIAL CONCERNS

1729–1738

Colden's first decade of residence at Coldengham, which was located about sixty miles from New York City, ninety miles from Albany, and a few miles from the west shore of the Hudson River, was characterized by a continuance of his involvement as an active surveyor general and provincial politician, both requiring frequent travel from home. He remained surveyor general until 1762, when he was replaced by his eldest son, Alexander. As a member of the Council there were trips to New York City, where he remained a highly visible figure. After October 1736, when present, Colden presided as the eldest councilor. Transportation between Coldengham and New York City was unpredictable and relied on sloops that sailed on the Hudson River between New York City and Albany. These vessels were sixty-five to seventy-five feet in length and had a limited number of cabin accommodations for the passengers. Schedules were unreliable due to the vagaries of wind and tide. When the river froze, travel ceased.

Concomitant with the move, Colden became a lessee and rented his house in New York City, using his close friend, James Alexander, as his agent. There is a record that among the renters, were a tavern keeper and a "jew," who "has no family but a wife & one servant & it would not Suit him to give any higher rent than £20 & the rest of the house besides your room [used for storage of Colden's books and goods] was Enough for him."[1]

The building of a permanent residence on the Coldengham estate in sparsely occupied Ulster County was a gradual and prolonged process. The kitchen was not completed until the fall of 1732.[2] At the time, Colden employed "4 Negro Men & two wenches and they all do their business cheerfully & seem contented."[3] Using Scottish stone masons, a three-story house with a stone exterior in Georgian style was built over several years. An addition was made between 1732 and 1733 to accommodate the increasing number in the family (fig. 4). The interior floors were made of planking, using local wood. Each of several rooms had a fireplace, perhaps adorned with Dutch tiles, stained paneling, and a decorated iron fireback.[4]

The Colden children performed a variety of chores, including collecting eggs, plucking feathers, and gathering fruits and nuts. The older girls carried out spinning, weaving, and sewing.[5] The estate contained an extensive orchard and nursery that included a variety of apples, cherries, pears, nectarines, and peaches.[6] Fried fish from the river were a staple of the diet. Oysters were also fired and oyster stew was a favorite dish.[7]

One of the unique aspects of the farm was the construction of a canal, which had its point of origin at an enlarged pond to allow shallow-draft barges to transport a variety of material on a stream that ran through the property.[8] The canal was identified during an archeological survey conducted in 1967, and is considered to be the first freshwater canal in the United States and the first to utilize horsepower to move boats along its course. Apparently, it began as a drainage ditch to eliminate a swamp, and was enlarged to allow for use by boats when Colden discovered deposits of peat or building-stone in the swamp.[9] Colden would later expand his canal concept, which was prescient for the development of the Erie Canal in the early nineteenth century. In a report to the Lords of Trade, he indicated that a direct link could be established between the Mohawk River and Lake Ontario and the other Great Lakes, "By which means of these Lakes & the Rivers which fall into them, Commerce may be carried from New York, through a vast Tract of Land, more easily than from any other maritime town in North America."[10] Colden extended his interests in the area almost immediately. He went into partnership with his neighbor Jacobus Bruyn and built a "publick house" at the Newburgh landing on the shore of the Hudson River, and leased it for £12 per year. He also set up a saw mill, which was functioning by 1731.[11]

Figure 4. Coldengham, woodcut from a map in the *New-York Historical Society Quarterly* XLV (July 1961). Courtesy of The New York Historical Society.

During the first decade at Coldengham, three more children were born (John on May 28, 1729; Catherine on February 13, 1731; and David on November 23, 1734). Maintenance of the farm and the education of his children occupied most of Colden's time when he was not away on business. But the children's education was mainly dependent on Mrs. Colden. A recollection of a descendent of Alice Colden provided a summation of her contribution to the family.

> In the remote situation of Coldengham . . . she performed the duties of a wife, mother and mistress with peculiar propriety. The management of every part of her family was initiated and admired by all who had just ideas and were similarly situated. . . . [T]his was fortunate for my Grandfather, whose superior genius for politics and philosophical pursuits rendered him indifferent to the management of household concerns—how happy was it for a man of his turn to be soon connected: I never saw more proof of the proper ascendancy of a husband, blended with esteem and love, than I have observed in this venerable Grand Mother, and I have often experienced how delightful it was to be an object of her affection. I have frequently heard those who have visited at the house observe, that the useful and agreeable qualities that should prevail everywhere, were by her judicious attentions very remarkably exhibited in those over which she had the direction, and when our intelligent progenitor, was called to preside over the government of New York, she did honor to his station by her conduct in every instance.[12]

Cadwallader was responsible for his son Alexander's preparation as a surveyor and his daughter Jane's development as a botanist. Alexander would perform his first survey as a twenty-one year old.[13] Latin was taught to the children by the local minister. In 1732, two of the older children, Alexander and Elizabeth, were sent to the city to enhance their education and social skills. This specifically included dancing school.

During the decade in question, the sole recorded correspondence of Colden related to the exchange of ideas was the February 1736 letter from William Douglass announcing the formation of a medical society in Boston and the society's preparation for publi-

cation of its first "Medical Memoirs," to include a history of a dys-
entery epidemic in Boston in 1734, and comments on the writings
of the famous seventeenth-century English physician, Thomas
Sydenham.[14]

Initially, Colden's time spent at the estate was probably devoted
to the improvement of the farm, the construction of the residence, and the education of the children. His frequent absences
from Coldengham, often of sufficient length to generate letters
between him and his wife, focused on his role as surveyor general
and his membership on the Council of the Province of New York.
The three-year period of Governor Montgomerie's stewardship of
the Province of New York generated little activity on the part of
the surveyor general's office. The governor had neither personal
interest in the acquisition of land grants nor the inclination to
satisfy the requests of others.

Under the governance of Montgomerie, in the three years of
his tenure, "The Governour's good humour too extinguished the
flames of contention, for being unable to plan, he had no particular
scheme to pursue; and thus by confining himself to the common
acts of government, our publick affairs flowed on in a peaceful
uninterrupted scheme."[15] In 1729, Montgomerie traveled to Albany
and on October 1 he renewed a treaty with the Six Nations and
gained their support for the defense of Oswego.[16] The year 1731 was
marked by the appearance of the first printed map of New York City,
the Lyne Survey (fig. 5) printed by William Bradford.

The death of Montgomerie on July 1, 1731, led to George
II's January 13, 1732 appointment of William Cosby as "Captain
General & Governor in Chief of the Provinces of New York,
New Jersey and Territories depending thereon in America."
Rip Van Dam, as the eldest councilman, was to serve as interim
governor. Cosby arrived in New York City with his family on
April 24, 1732, and assumed office on August 2. Colden's situ-
ation changed substantially under the stewardship of Cosby.

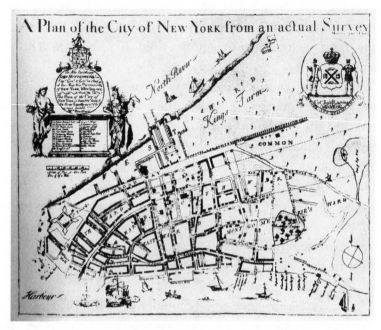

Figure 5. James Lyne, A Plan of the City of New York from an actual Survey" 1731, printed by William Bradford, New York. Engraving, 45 x 57 cm. Courtesy of Rare Book Division, New York Public Library, Astor, Lenox and Tilden Foundations.

Governor Cosby has been portrayed as one of the most egocentric and oppressive governors in all of British Colonial America's history. Cosby's arrival at New York immediately altered the political scene and created extreme polarization that affected every major political figure. Cosby's supporters included George Clarke, Archibald Kennedy, Adolph Philipse, Philip Van Cortland, and James Delancey, whom Cosby named chief justice after removing Lewis Morris from office. The group constituted the court party, which was more cosmopolitan, favoring trade with the French at Montreal and overseas trade. Colden's closest confidants—Lewis Morris, James Alexander, Rip Van Dam, and William Smith—led the competitive country party, which focused on provincial economic development and constituted Cosby's political foes.

Cosby's self-interest was also blatantly manifest. He demanded that the late acting governor, Rip Van Dam, remit half his salary to Cosby, and demanded a third of every land patent grant, in addition to petitioning for major grants for himself. Within two years of his arrival, patents were issued for 15,000; 27,000; and 86,000 acres. Cosby asked for 48,000 acres for himself.[17] In 1734, Cosby received a land grant from the king of 22,000 acres on the Mohawk River in what became Herkimer County.

Colden represented an obstruction to Cosby's land acquisition, and the governor moved to remove Colden from office. Daniel Horsmanden, a young scheming lawyer, whom Cosby had appointed to the Council much to the dismay of several councilors, maintained a friendly relationship with Colden, in part for personal gains of land. In a letter to Colden, dated November 19, 1734, Horsmanden informed his friend:

> Our friend Mathews yesterday Surprized me with an Acco[t] That on Saturday Evening last You were suspended from your Office of Survey Gen[ll]. If it be tru, 'twas done in Such privacy, that I know not one Syllable of it.

Lewis Morris, who had been deposed from his position as chief justice by Governor Cosby, wrote to the Marquis of Lothian in defense of Colden.[18] Lewis pointed out that the duty of the surveyor general was not only to survey lands granted by the Crown and insure that the grantees do not overstep their privilege but also to prevent the governors from granting land in a manner other than the Crown intended. Thus the surveyor general, in effect, was to restrain a governor in his pursuit of personal gain.

In the letter, Morris continued that it was probably Colden's restraint of Cosby's aggrandizement of land that rendered Colden an inimical personality for the governor rather than the three purported criticisms, which had circulated from the governor's camp. The first of the governor's criticisms indicated that Colden openly stated that the governor's bills had been protested openly by Colden. This never occurred. The second claimed that Colden had revealed secrets of the Council. This was also untrue. The third proposed that Colden was a Jacobite. This was refuted by the previously referred to action of Colden at Kelso in 1715 (see p. 16). As it turned out, Colden was never suspended, and maintained his position throughout Cosby's governorship and for years thereafter.

In his role as surveyor general, Colden's expertise was invoked to establish the boundaries between adjacent colonies. Although the boundary between Connecticut and New York was established in 1664, it remained uncontested until 1684. At that time, Connecticut began to dispute the jurisdiction of several towns within the territory concerning jurisdiction. A tentative agreement between the two colonies was reached in 1725.[19] Colden had been an active participant on that occasion. The more recent focal point of disagreement, concerning the rights of the citizens of Richfield, was settled and articles of agreement were signed on May 18, 1732.[20] In 1737, Colden served on the commission for settling the boundary between Massachusetts and New Hampshire.[21] In 1741, also Colden served on the commission to define the boundary between Massachusetts and Rhode Island.[22]

With Governor Cosby's arrival, Colden's political contributions were significantly minimized. Colden's deliberate absence from the Council meetings was a factor. He revealed his sentiments regarding his political status in a letter to his Aunt Elizabeth Hill in January 1734.

> It is too true what you hear of the uneasiness the people of this province are under at this time. There is a Complaint gone home against the Governor & probably by next spring it will be known what effect it is like to have As to my part I cannot value my self upon any great share in the Governour's friendship & for that

reason I cannot place any security in it but it is said to be some comfort to have many under the same misfortune. However the distance I am at from New York frees me from a good deal of uneasiness that could not be avoided were I there at this time. My endeavor shall be to maintain the Character of an honest man & while I do that I hope never to forfeit your esteem & love It will be the greatest support & comfort to me under what ever misfortunes may be fall me I have taken all the measures which I think prudent to guard against any attempt that may be made & I hope they will be successful but they will create me some experience.[23]

Although a friend of the governor suggested that it was desirable for the governor to "create an intimate Friendship with you [Colden], because I knew he had much to expect from the Friendship of Man, with your Knowledge of the Nature of the Government, and of the Temper, and different Inclinations of the People he was to govern."[24] This never came to pass.

Colden was a peripheral participant in what was arguably the most significant and most referred to legal trial and decision in the history of British Colonial America. The trial of John Peter Zenger can be traced back to the arrival of Governor Cosby. On his arrival at New York, Cosby disputed the allocation of funds for the salary of Rip Van Dam, the chairman of the Council and acting governor after Montgomerie's death. To resolve the argument to his advantage, Cosby established a chancery court. Chief Justice Lewis Morris objected, based on the fact that the jurisdiction for such a court had expired and that there had been no act by either the Parliament or the Assembly to empower such a court. Governor Cosby responded by dismissing Morris from the position of chief justice and appointing James Delancey to the post. Lewis Morris and his son, Lewis, Jr., then ran for seats representing Westchester County in the New York Assembly and won.

They spearheaded the establishment the *New-York Weekly Journal*, a newspaper to express views in opposition to those of Cosby and his confidants, which appeared in the city's only existing periodical, William Bradford's *Gazette*. The *New-York Weekly Journal* was edited by James Alexander, Colden's close friend. It emphasized praise for Lewis Morris and criticism of Governor Cosby and his policies. In addition to accusing the governor of an assortment of misconducts, the editorial material accused his government of illegal elections and permitting the French navy to explore New York harbor.

On November 2, 1734, Colden was a member of a privy council that met at Fort George, New York, and ordered that certain issues of the *New-York Weekly Journal* were to be burned "by the common hangman or whipper, near the pillory in this city, on Wednesday the 6th. . . ."[25] The governor declared the journal to be scandalous, and endorsed the order for the papers to be burned. Zenger was arrested for seditious libel on November 17, 1734. James Alexander and William Smith, who were lawyers within the opposition to the governor, were excluded from the court by the chief justice. As the trial was to begin in July 1735, the supporters of the printer were pessimistic about the outcome.

A Philadelphia lawyer named Andrew Hamilton was engaged by the defense. He established that a jury rather than the chief justice would decide if the published statements were true or false, and, if true they should not be considered libelous. The jury was convinced that the newspaper's statements were true and returned a verdict of "not guilty." The citizens of the city celebrated and Hamilton was presented with "the freedom of the city in a gold box on which were inscribed . . . Demersae leges—time facta libertas—haec tandem emergunt"[26] (the laws being submerged—and liberty made fearful—these emerge at last). The judgment established the precedent for freedom of the press in America by declaring that a printed defamatory statement, which is proved to be true, is not libelous.

Despite Colden's endorsement of the burning of issues of the *New York Weekly Post*, he remained more closely allied with

Lewis Morris, James Alexander, and the group that favored the landowners rather than the merchants and Governor Cosby. But, Colden's physical absence from the eye of political storms allowed him to maintain a somewhat detached appearance rather than that of the champion of a cause.

Colden was made aware of Governor Cosby's rapidly advancing illness toward the end of 1735.[27] The governor died on March 10, 1736, of what was likely tuberculosis. The populace was exultant while the politicians had mixed feelings about his successor.[28] Traditionally, Rip Van Dam, as senior councilor, would have become the acting governor. But, because Van Dam was suspended from the Council when Cosby became ill, George Clarke assumed the leadership role. A contentious period of anarchy ensued and lasted until October when Clarke received notification from the government in England naming him as president and commander-in-chief of the province. This was strengthened by his advancement to the rank of lieutenant governor at the end of the month.[29]

Colden sent the newly instated lieutenant governor a letter, dated November 3 and written while he was surveying Mohawk lands for purchase, that he signed "your Honours and most Obedient & most humble Serv[t.]"[30] as confirmation of his desire to establish a harmonious relationship. Although Colden maintained a close association with James Alexander, Lewis Morris, and William Smith, Sr., as political allies, who represented the minority faction, Colden was also able to enjoy collegiality with Clarke, his former antagonist.

At the beginning of Clarke's period of leadership, Chief Justice Delancey and Adolph Philipse swayed the Council, while the opposition led by Lewis Morris, his son, Lewis, Jr., and James Alexander directed the Assembly. As a consequence, the election that took place in 1737 was particularly contentious. In the course of events leading up to the vote, the votes by Jewish inhabitants were disallowed and for about a decade the Jews were disfranchised.[31]

That same year witnessed the beginning of a situation, in which Lieutenant Governor Clarke and Surveyor General Colden were allied and eventually became the subjects of censure. Their action evoked criticism that would mature into a cause célèbre. Both Clarke and Colden believed in encouraging settlements, consisting of farms and estates, along the frontier to counter encroachment by the French in Canada. Governor Cosby had previously proclaimed that 100,000 acres near Lake George was to be made available to immigrant Protestant families. Clarke and Colden were initially pleased with the proposal by Captain Laughlin Campbell to form a feudal estate on that frontier land with about eighty Scottish families. It turned out that Campbell lacked the financial resources to fund his scheme and the families, who came as part of the endeavor, were unwilling to participate under the leadership of Campbell. They applied for land on which they could create separate farms, but the patent for the land was withheld. Colden's refusal to allow the settlers to acquire parcels of land generated widespread criticism that affected his reputation for the remainder of his life.

The criticism reached its peak in 1757 with the publication of volume one of William Smith, Jr.'s *The History of the Province of New-York*. The author, whose book was published when he was only twenty-nine years old, was the son of a distinguished New York lawyer. The senior Smith was made attorney general of New York in 1751, and from 1753 until 1757 he was a member of the Council. During the 1730s and 1740s, the senior Smith and Colden were friends and allied in opposition to Adolph Philipse and James Delancey. In the 1750s, the relationship between Smith, Sr., and Colden transformed into bitter hatred.[32]

The title page of the first volume of William Smith, Jr.'s book specifies "From the First Discovery to the Year 1732." In the first volume, the final pages of history, "Part V: From the Year 1720 to the Commencement of the Administration of Colonel Cosby

(1732)" extends the time frame by bringing into focus the episode related to Colden that took place in 1737.

> Captain Laughlin Campbel, encouraged by a proclamation to that purpose, came over in 1737, and ample promises were made to him. He went upon the land, viewed it and approved it; and was entreated to settle there, even by the Indians, who were taken with his Highland dress, Mr. Clarke, the Lieutenant Governour, promised him, in a printed advertisement, the grant of 30,000 acres of land, free from all but charges of the survey and the King's quit rent. Confiding on the faith of the government, Captain Campbel, went home to Isla, sold his estate, and, shortly after, transported, at his own expense, 83 Protestant families, consisting of 423 adults, besides a great number of children. Private faith and publick honour loudly demanded the fair execution of the project, so expensive to the undertaker and beneficial to the colony. *But it unfortunately dropped, through the sordid views of some persons in power, who aimed at a share in the intended grant; to which Campbel, who was a man of spirit, would not consent.* [my italics][33]

In fact, Smith's interpretation was a misrepresentation, which he could have avoided by consulting contemporary records. Campbell should have been aware that the 100,000 acres had already been allocated. He had only been promised "sufficient land" for as many settlers as he attracted at three pounds per hundred acres and the annual quit rent to the Crown. Campbell had refused the 19,000 acres offered to him and also had falsely included in his list of settlers several who had been in New York before he arrived. Campbell's scheme was aborted because of his own personal greed and determination to make tenants of the settlers.[34]

Chapter 4

CONCENTRATED CORRESPONDENCE AND EVOLVING ENLIGHTENMENT

1739-1748

*T*his decade best reflects the multifaceted aspects of Colden's life. Because he was well established in his country estate and more often distant from the disturbing aspects of city life, he was able to focus on his intellectual pursuits and devote an increased amount of time to an extensive correspondence with an array of individuals with similar interests. The colonies offered a limited number of intellectuals who gained his respect. Letters to and from Dr. John Mitchell introduced another medical association to his life. Benjamin Franklin and Colden exchanged letters on a variety of subjects, while the correspondence with Dr. Samuel Johnson gave vent to philosophical and metaphysical interests. John Bartram shared an interest in botany. The paucity of Americans who were held in high regard by Colden necessitated frequent transatlantic correspondence. The names of Carolus Linnaeus and Johnannes Frederick Gronovius joined that of Peter Collinson as correspondents with the common interest of botany.

The early part of the decade continued to require Colden's multiple and, at times, prolonged absences from his family and the tranquility of Coldengham, as he exercised his roles of surveyor general and provincial Councilman. Colden had hoped to spend more time on a revision of *The History of the Five Indian Nations*, but, as he wrote to Collinson, the project was "entirely laid a side by reason that my Business carrying me from home almost three quarters of the year. . . ."[1]

The position of surveyor general was time consuming. In August 1748, Governor Clinton chronicled that Colden had served as surveyor general for about twenty-eight years, all but three without a salary from the province. In that position, Colden was compensated only by fees from those who received grants of land that required survey. An annual salary of one hundred pounds sterling was suggested.[2] During the decade under consideration, Colden conducted several surveys and was appointed in December 1740 to serve on a commission to determine the boundaries between the Province of Massachusetts Bay and the Colony of Rhode Island that was held in April of the following year.[3]

Related to surveying, Colden devised a new and more exact quadrant to determine distance more accurately utilizing a micrometer screw. He submitted the plans to Collinson to have it evaluated by a machinist in England. It was deemed to be flawed and impractical.[4]

With the workings on his farm stabilized and his involvement in political affairs temporarily reduced, Colden was able to rekindle his interest in botany. In 1741, Collinson informed Colden that he should anticipate a visit from the individual who was internationally regarded to be the American colonies' leading botanist, "an Ingenious Man and a great teacher unto Nature Named John Bartram of Pensilvania. . . ."[5] Bartram was a native Pennsylvanian, whom Linnaeus held in the highest esteem. Bartram was a farmer without formal education but was driven by a lifelong interest in botany, particularly plants with medicinal applications. He has been assigned the designation of the "father of American Botany."

Bartram travelled extensively in the eastern colonies collecting plants and chronicled his observations in publications, *Observations on the Inhabitants, Climate, Soil, Rivers, Productions, Animals, and other Matters Worthy of Notice, made by Mr. John Bartram in his Travels from Pennsylvania to Onondaga, Oswego, and the Lake Ontario, in Canada* (London, 1751), and *Diary of a Journey through the Carolinas, Georgia, and Florida* (American Philosophical Society Transactions, XXXIII, 1942). Bartram had forwarded many of the plant specimens that he collected to Linnaeus, Gronovius, and other European botanical taxonomists. Bartram's life and Colden's would intersect over decades and it was probably Bartram who proposed Colden for membership in the American Philosophical Society sometime after June 1744.[6]

Shortly following Bartram's visit to Coldengham, Colden wrote Collinson, "Few in America have and tasted in Botany and still fewer if any of these have ability to form & keep a Botanical Garden without which it is impracticable to give compleat Characters of Plants. In short I may positively assert that not one in America has both the power & the will for such a performance."[7]

In 1742, Colden became acquainted with *Genera Plantarum*, which Linnaeus, the Swedish father of a system of taxonomy based on the sexual characteristics of plants, had published in 1737. As Colden wrote over a decade later, "About the year 1742 a student from Leiden gave me the perusal of Dr Linnaeus Characters of Plants As his Method was new to me & appeared exceedingly curious & his characters more accurate than any I had seen it excited my curiosity to examine the plants which grew around my house I put my observations in writing As I was an unexpert botanist I was in doubt whether I had reduced the plants to their proper genera & some of them I was not able to reduce to any Genus in the book For this reason I sent my Observations to Dr Gronovius in Leiden."[8] In 1743, Colden received his first of many letters from Johannes Frederick Gronovius, the Leiden botanist and patron of Linnaeus, who would continue to supply Colden with the sequential publications of Linnaeus.[9]

Bartram was impressed with Colden and wrote to Collinson that "this hath been A happy journey & I met with our friend doctor Colden who received & entertained me with all ye demonstrations of civility & respect that was Convenient He is one of the most facetious agreeable gentlemen I have ever met. . . ."[10] Colden and Bartram continued to exchange plant specimens over the years.

In keeping with Colden's critical nature and his need to provide his own input in formulating broad concepts (as was the case for his consideration of Newtonian physics) he suggested that there were faults with Linnaeus's sexual system of plant classification, and proposed a system based on small steps of Natural Gradation.[11] Colden constructed a catalogue, using the Linnaean system, of the flora in the vicinity of Coldengham. Linnaeus published the catalogue as "Plantae Coldenhamiae in provincia Novaboracensi Americanes sponte Crescentes."[12] When Linnaeus published *Species Plantarum* in 1753 he referred to "C. Colden" as a source of his knowledge of New World flora. Colden's name would become a permanent part of botanical taxonomy when Linnaeus, in *Flora Zeylanica,* assigned *Coldenia* to a specific plant, a genus of borginaceous herb of the species *Ehreticoe,* and Colden was honored with the title of *Summus Perfectus.*

In appreciation of Colden's reputation, Benjamin Franklin wrote him: "I congratulate you on the Immortality conferr'd on you by the learned Naturalists of Europe. No Species or Genus of Plants was ever lost, or ever will be while the World Continues; and, therefore your Name, now annext to one of them, will last forever."[13]

Colden's relationship with Benjamin Franklin was initiated during this decade. According to a letter that Colden wrote to William Strahan, he met Franklin in the summer of 1743 while traveling. Colden related, "I accidentally last summer fell into Company with a Printer (the most ingenious in his way without question of any in America . . .)."[14] Between 1743 and 1748 he wrote two letters to Franklin. Colden first submitted to Franklin his work on Fluxions, and the Different Species of Matter for comments and evaluation by the Philadelphia savant, James Logan.[15] Colden subsequently requested Franklin's assistance in the purchase of a newly designed apparatus for electrical experiments.[16]

During the same period, fifteen letters from Benjamin Franklin to Cadwallader are recorded. The first recorded instance of the extensive correspondence between Franklin and Colden is dated November 4, 1743, and consists of Franklin's response to a letter from Colden in which the latter proposed a new method of printing known as stereotyping.[17] It was subsequently deemed impractical by Will Strahan, the London printer, who sent one of his journey men, David Hall, to manage Benjamin Franklin's Philadelphia printing establishment.[18] Franklin also related Logan's criticisms of Colden's paper on Fluxions.[19] In another letter to Colden regarding his conclusions about perspiration and absorption through the skin, Franklin offered his own speculations.[20]

In a 1746 letter from Franklin to Colden, there appeared Franklin's initial attempt to determine why ships sailing from the colonies to England took significantly less time than the reverse voyage. Franklin initially ascribed the phenomenon to the diurnal motion of earth.[21] Colden opined that the shorter voyages to Europe were due to the effects of tides and contrary currents when sailing westerly.[22] More than twenty years later, the first printed chart of the Gulf Stream appeared. It was brought about through the efforts of Franklin, who was then serving as deputy postmaster general for the American colonies. Based on the knowledge that the stream was a current of warm water, Franklin provided his nephew, Timothy Folger, with a thermometer to measure the water's temperature and chart the Gulf Stream during a voyage. In another letter to Colden, Franklin made mention of the stove that he devised to increase the generation of heat.[23]

Franklin also indicated that he had read the 1747 edition of Colden's book, *The History of the Five Indian Nations*, and he wrote, "I can only tell you my own Opinion that 'tis a well wrote, entertaining & instructive Piece, and must be exceedingly usefull to all those Colonies who have anything to do with Indian Affairs."[24]

Colden's name joins that of Franklin on the early roster of members of the American Philosophical Society, for which Franklin is credited as the proposer. Colden's relationship with the society, America's oldest learned society, might be dated to the spring of 1743 when Colden met Benjamin Franklin by chance on the road while travelling in New England.[25] It is highly probable that they discussed the development of a learned society in the colonies. In Franklin's November 4, 1743 letter to Colden, he indicated that he "had no Leisure to forward the Scheme of the Society: But that Hurry being now near over, I purpose to proceed in the affair very soon, your Approbation being no small Encouragement to me."[26]

As noted previously (see p. 32), in 1728, Colden had indicated to William Douglass the need for such a learned society in the colonies. In 1743, John Bartram and Benjamin Franklin circulated among their friends and correspondents "A PROPOSAL for Promoting USEFUL KNOWLEDGE among the British Plantations in America." Although it was printed by Franklin's press as a broadside bearing Franklin's signature, there are indications that the project was a joint product of Franklin's and Bartram's efforts.[27] Nine Philadelphians constituted the core of the society that was established and three meetings were held in 1744. In April of that year, seven new members were initiated, of whom Colden was elected by unanimous consent.[28] Both Colden and Mitchell visited Philadelphia after their election to membership.[29]

Shortly thereafter, the society lapsed into inactivity, at which point, Franklin indicated a plan to proceed with publishing papers,[30] a suggestion that Colden had previously made to him.[31] The society was eventually revived in 1767 and in 1769 it united with the American Society for Promoting and Propagating Useful Knowledge and Benjamin Franklin was elected the first president. Colden's name remained on the roll of members at the time that the unification occurred. Although he never attended a meeting, about thirty years after his election, some of his "remarks on some obvious Phenomena of Light" were presented to the members.[32]

During the decade, Colden maintained his interest in medical matters. In 1741, his *Essay on the Iliac Passion* was printed by Benjamin Franklin. As a physician, Colden's attention was drawn to public health issues in New York City and the need to improve sanitation. In 1743 and 1744, James Parker printed, in New York, articles by Colden on seasonal fevers that affected citizens of the city while sparing those who lived in rural areas. James Alexander, Colden's fellow councilman and closest friend, informed Colden that "the paper I believe & hope has had the Effect to witt to Convince a majority of our Magistrates of the necessity of removing Skinners Tanners &c to fresh water & Either cleaning or filling up the Slips before Summer and measures are taking for doing these things & putting their former Laws as to the keeping clean the Streets & docks is better Execution—All whom I have talkt to on this head think themselves & the City very much obliged to you."[33]

Colden was especially critical of the contamination of stagnant water in the area of the docks, and he urged that removal of the filth and better drainage be carried out. He insisted that the responsibility be assigned to a tax-supported entity rather than contracted to private parties.[34] As a consequence of Colden's efforts, which gain him primacy as the first to deal with public health in the Province of New York, corrective measures were undertaken and more stringent regulations were adopted.[35]

Colden's medical notes chronicle his observations on the bite of a rattle snake that injected its venom into a steer. Successful treatment was effected by pouring heated hog's lard down the throat into the stomach of the steer.[36] He speculated on the relationship between Yaws and Lues Venera, and indicated that the former had an African origin while the latter originated in America before the European explorers arrived, thereby making the two distinct species of disease.[37] Colden's treatise on Tar water, *An Abstract from Dr. Berkeley's Treatise on Tar-Water with Some Reflections Thereon, Adapted to Diseases Frequent in America,* was printed by James Parker in 1744.[38]

A common interest in medicine brought Colden together with John Mitchell, who became a member of the American Philosophical Society at the same time as Colden. The relationship began in June 1745 with an introductory letter from Colden to Mitchell, and continued when Franklin sent Colden Mitchell's reflections about pestilential distemper (Yellow Fever) in accordance with Mitchell's request.[39] For a disease that was associated with 90 percent mortality, Mitchell recommended diaphoretics and purgatives to stimulation evacuation. In reference to the treatment of pleurisy and pneumonia, Mitchell introduced the new medicine, named Rattlesnake Root (*Polygala senega*).[40]

In Colden's letter of response to Mitchell, he reported on the epidemics of 1743 and 1745 in New York City. He ascribed the disease to importation from England, Europe, and the West Indies because it that is where it first appeared and was concentrated near the docks. It is now felt that the "Yellow Fever," which gained the attention of many colonial physicians, including the most notable Benjamin Rush, was probably either infectious hepatitis or Weil's disease (food or water contaminated by urine containing *Leptospira icterohaemorhagiae* of infected rats).[41] Colden included reports of the benefits of Tar Water as treatment of Yaws, gout, and scurvy. In that letter Colden deviated from medicine to bring into focus his own intellectual accomplishments in Newtonian science.[42]

> I think I have discover'd the first principles of Action in the Material World & that I can demonstrate them & from them demonstrate not only all the Phenomena arising from Gravitation

but the cause of Gravitation itself In short I think I can demonstrate the Theorem in Sr Isaac Newtones Principia from these Principles & that independently from the conic sections which alone would be of some advantage to those who would not be so perfect in that Doctrine as the understanding of Sr Isaac Principia requires. . . . I am in hopes it may likewise be of use to explain some other Phenomena besides Gravitation of which none of the Philosophers have hitherto been able to give any tolerable account."[43]

JOHN MITCHELL

John Mitchell, with whom Cadwallader Colden never made personal contact, shared with Colden the status of an Edinburgh trained colonial physician, a concern with the Anglo-French rivalry in North America, cartography of the pertinent region, a continued interest in botany, as well as early membership in the American Philosophical Society.

Unlike his contemporary medical colleagues, Colden and Douglass, John Mitchell was a native American, born in White Chapel Parish, Lancaster County, Virginia, on April 13, 1711. He was the son of a comfortable planter and merchant. As a young teen, Mitchell was sent to Edinburgh, which awarded him a master's degree in 1729. While at the university he studied botany under Dr. Charles Alston, who later became the King's Botanist for Scotland. Over the ensuing two years, Mitchell continued his studies in preparation for a career in medicine. He enrolled in the anatomy course of Alexander Monro *primus* and the class on the practice of medicine conducted by John Rutherfurd, the grandfather of Sir Walter Scott. Mitchell did not receive a medical degree, but returned home to practice medicine in Lancaster for two years before moving to Urbanna in Middlesex County, Virginia, where he spent his remaining years in America.[44]

Mitchell maintained his interest in botany and began collecting plant specimens from his region almost immediately after his return to Virginia. He shared these with his fellow Virginian John Clayton who assembled "A Catalogue of Plants, Fruits and Trees Native to Virginia," which was dispatched to Dr. Johannes Frederick Gronovius who, without Clayton's knowledge or permission, published the material in 1739 with the title of *Flora Virginica*.[45]

As early as 1737, John Mitchell began his correspondence with Peter Collinson, the conduit between colonial botanists and those with shared interests in Great Britain and Europe. The only surviving letter between the two was dated March 11, 1741. It included Mitchell's taxonomic treatise and descriptions of thirty new floral genera.[46] Collinson forwarded the treatise to Christopher Jacob Trew in Nuremberg who had it published in the proceedings of the local academy in 1748.[47] Thus, Mitchell is credited as the first North American to publish on taxonomy.[48]

At the same time that he collected plant specimens in Virginia, Mitchell, in response to the curiosity of Peter Collinson and other Englishmen, studied and dissected both male and female opossums. The findings were read at a meeting of the Royal Society of London on February 10, 1743.[49] Mitchell's first publication appeared in the *Philosophical Transactions* of the Royal Society in 1744. The paper was a consideration of the causes of different pigmentations in people. Mitchell deduced from his own studies of the composition of Negro skin:

> From what has been said about the Cause of the Colour of black and white People we may justly conclude, that they might very naturally be both descended from one and the same Parents, as we are better assured from Scripture, that they are. . . . For the different Colours of People have been demonstrated to be only the necessary Effects, and natural Consequences, of their respective Climes and Ways of Life; as we may further learn from Experience, that they are the most suitable for the Preservation of Health, and the Ease and Convenience of mankind in the

Climes and Ways of Living: So that the black Colour of the Negroes of *Africa*, instead of being a Curse denounced on them, on account of their Forefather *Ham*, as some have idly imagined, is rather a Blessing, rendering their lives in that intemperate Region, more tolerable, and less painful. . . .[50]

Mitchell met Bartram and Franklin during a visit to Philadelphia in 1744. This stimulated the initiation of correspondence between Mitchell and Colden. In September of the next year, Mitchell wrote to Franklin about his deteriorating health, manifested by fever, diarrhea, "Piles," and spitting of blood.[51] Unable to continue practicing medicine and because he attributed part of his disability to the climate of Virginia, Mitchell sold his house and possessions, including his library and sailed for England with his wife in the beginning of 1746, reaching London in May.

Mitchell and Colden continued to correspond. Knowing of their mutual admiration, Collinson, who was engaged in having a second edition of Colden's *History of the Five Indian Nations* published, asked Mitchell to draw up a new title page.[52] Mitchell spent a significant effort on the project, only to learn from Colden, two years after the 1747 publication, that he was displeased because the English edition was dedicated to General James Edward Ogelthorpe, a trustee of the colony of Georgia, with whom Colden had no acquaintance.[53]

Mitchell was elected to the Royal Society in December 1748 as "A Gentleman of great merit and Learning, who . . . from his great application to the Study of Natural History, especially Botany, is very well acquainted with the Vegetable production of North America." His accomplishment in Botany was further honored by Linnaeus in the 1753 publication of *Species Plantarum*, in which the partridge berry was given the name *Mitchella repens*.

As the subtitle of the definitive biography of Dr. John Mitchell indicates, he is best remembered as "The Man who made the Map of North America."[54] Mitchell, like Colden, was deeply concerned with the threat of French expansion in North America. The Lords Commissioners of Trade and Plantation appreciated the need to delineate British and French claims, particularly related to lands in the Ohio Valley and west of the British colonies whose boundaries were poorly defined. The French were producing maps on which their claims were staked and the British needed to rebut those claims. This was complicated by that fact that the only previous large-scale map, which was made by Henry Popple in 1733, had many errors and failed to display facts and boundaries appropriate for consideration.

The Lords Commissioners were apparently acquainted with a map of North America that Mitchell had produced in 1750.[55] Consequently Mitchell was retained to create a new and improved map based on up-to-date material provided by each of the colonial governors. The result was the 1755 publication of Mitchell's "A Map of the British and French Dominions in North America with the Roads, Distances, Limits, and Extent of the Settlements." Twenty-one editions and impressions of Mitchell's map appeared in four languages between 1755 and 1781. Copies of the third edition of the map were used by John Jay, John Adams, and Benjamin Franklin during the negotiations for the 1783 Treaty of Paris at the end of the Revolutionary War when the boundaries of the United States and Canada were defined. The map was referred to in boundary disputes throughout the eighteenth and nineteenth century and most recently in 1932.[56]

The high regard that John Mitchell enjoyed in London is attested to by his selection as one of two candidates for the position of keeper of the newly created British Museum. After two and a half years of deliberation, the alternate candidate, Gowin Knight, was selected by King George II in 1758.[57] One year before the selection, *The Contest in America between Great Britain and France with Its Consequence and Importance* was published by the same man who printed Mitchell's map. There is little doubt that Mitchell was the author of that work, which was directed at making the colonies better valued and pointing out the dangers the French, currently on the North American continent, represented.[58]

In 1759, Mitchell moved to Kew in order to become an active participant in the formation of the Royal Botanic Gardens, which had been initiated by the Prince of Wales and supported by Mitchell's intimate friend, the Earl of Bute. In 1767, Mitchell's *Present State of Great Britain and North America with regard to Agriculture, Population, Trade, and Manufactures, impartially considered* was published in London. He considered the 1765 Stamp Act to have been unwise and stressed that imposing taxed on the colonies was counterproductive to their desired expansion. Mitchell died in London on February 29, 1768, in the same month that his membership in the revived American Philosophical Society was confirmed.[59]

* * *

In the early 1740s, Colden was able to dedicate much of his time at Coldengham to his favorite intellectual subject, a consideration of Isaac Newton's postulates regarding matter, motion, and gravitation. Newton's *Principia Mathematica,* in which his three universal laws of motion appeared, was published in 1697. The First Law states that an object at rest tends to stay at rest and an object in uniform motion tends to stay in motion unless acted upon by an external net force. The Second Law states that an applied force on an object equals the rate of change of its momentum with time. These two laws indicate that a force is only needed in order to change an object's state of motion. Newton's Third Law states that for every action there is an equal and opposite reaction.

Colden's initial exposure to Newtonian science occurred during his course in physics at the University of Edinburgh. His notes provide evidence of the awe with which he regarded Newton's work.[60] As Colden continued his interest in Newtonian science, the genesis of his publication was his sincere conviction that his understanding of the science was sufficient for him to make meaningful improvements. As Colden wrote to Peter Collinson in June 1745:

> I had pleased myself with the conceit of my being able to explain the Cause of Gravitation a point which has hitherto puzzled the ablest of Philosophers. My speculations have so far pleas'd my self & appear to me to be founded upon such evident principles that I have adventur'd to put them to the press in order to have a sufficient number of copies to submit it to the examination of the Learned. . . . As a meer point of Speculation I think it will be acceptable to the curious if it in any manner approach to the opinion I have of it. . . . [I]t opens a Method for improvement in Astronomy & all the Sciences which depend on it as Navigation & Geography which exceeds anything done hitherto. . . . I propose to give an entire Theory of the Earth's motion from the Principles in this treatise which I have now published which in several parts will be entirely new. I propose to explain the Phenomena from those principles & some of which tho principal Phenomena in the earths motion not so much as attempted by S[r] Isa. New[t]. . . ."[61]

Colden considered himself qualified to disagree with some of Newton's postulates. He wrote to Samuel Johnson requesting an opinion of his treatise: "You will find by some parts of that piece that tho' I have the greatest esteem of S[r] Isaac Newtons knowledge & performances I take the liberty to differ from him in some points That man never existed that never err'd."[62]

Newton had formulated laws by which the effects of gravitation could be predicted, but he specifically indicated that he could not define the cause. He wrote, "I have not been able to discover the cause of the properties of gravity from [the observation of] phenomena and I frame no hypotheses."[63]

Unlike Newton, who specifically based his analyses on observations and experimentations, Colden eschewed inductive reasoning and based his conclusions on unsubstantiated hypotheses.

Colden's hypotheses were mainly in keeping with the sections entitled "General Scholium" at the end of Newton's *Principia* and "Queries" at the end of *Optics*, in which Newton indulged himself in speculation. These sections were in distinct variance with Newton's expression of his theses, which were based on reasoning, careful experimentation, and mathematical calculations. Colden had failed to comprehend Newton's concept of inertia, his laws of motion, or the balances of forces exerted upon the planets.[64] As a result, a historical assessment has declared: "No more audacious claim to intellectual eminence was ever made in colonial America than Cadwallader Colden's assertion, in the middle of the eighteenth century, that he had discovered the cause of gravitation."[65]

Colden's explanation of gravity had as its basis the division of the material of the world into three distinct substances: *ether, resisting matter,* and *moving matter.* Colden followed the concept of Newton by invoking *ether* as the medium that was responsible for pushing bodies together and accounting for gravity. Colden also defined *ether* as "a subtile elastic fluid exceedingly more subtile and elastic than common air,"[66] Colden's *ether* "fills every space, not occupied by resisting matter, and so, consequently, permeates all the interstices between the parts or particles, which compose bodies of inert or resisting matter."[67]

As an explanation for gravitation, Newton proposed that the ether had a varied density, which was increased as the distance from a body increased. Attraction was a result the movement of a body from denser parts to rarer parts of the medium. Newton admitted uncertainty of this hypothesis and stated that he did not know what ether was. Colden's *ether* was a distinctly different entity, which he defined without hesitation. His *ether* possessed a constant density, without any distance between points within it, and it did not extend throughout space. Most irreconcilable was the hypothesis that two bodies in *ether* encountered less force on the sides facing each other than on all other sides because there was less ether between them than surrounding them. The resultant force brought the bodies together. Thus, Colden concluded that gravitation was caused by the "reaction" of ether on bodies of matter.[68]

Colden borrowed the term "matter" from Newton and referred to bodies having mass and occupying space as *resisting matter*. He followed Newton in asserting that the innate force in matter is the power to resist, equating resistance with inertia. A body at rest continues at rest, while a body in motion continues moving uniformly unless a force is applied. Resistance, according to Colden, was active rather than passive, as was the case for Newton. Colden's third form of matter was termed *moving matter*, which was essentially Newton's corpuscular light, namely, light made up of small discrete particles called "corpuscles," which travel in a straight line with a finite velocity and possess kinetic energy. To light Colden ascribed the sole power of movement in the universe. Bodies in motion must continually receive new energy from light or motion would decrease and cease.

In Colden's universe, gravity was the force exerted by *ether* upon the planets and stars. There were fewer ether particles between the sun and each of the planets than between planets. This resulted in a force that would cause each planet to move toward the sun. Counteracting that force were light particles emanating from the sun. Light constituted the sole power of movement in the universe. It was responsible for the planets' orbits, their orbital velocities, and also the rotations of planets on their axes.

The earliest evidence of Colden's attention to the extension of Newton's work is the manuscript *An Introduction to the Doctrine of Fluxions* (calculus), which Colden disseminated to several of his correspondents, including John Rutherfurd,[69] Alexander, Franklin, and Logan in 1743. Colden wrote to Collinson that he was directing his attention away from botany to a subject "so bold that I dare not trouble you with it or even to mention the subject till it has undergone the examination of some Friends here."[70]

As mentioned previously, Franklin was one of the recipients of Colden's manuscript, which he shared with Logan. Franklin responded:

> I communicated your Piece of Fluxions to Mr Logan, and being in his House a few Days after, he told me, he had read it cursorily, that he thought you had not fully hit the Matter, and (*I think*) that Berkeley's Objections were well founded; but said he would read it over more attentively. Since that, he tells me there are several Mistakes in it, two of which he mark'd on Page 10. He says X X is by no Means = X + X nor is the square of 10 + 1 + 10:2:01 but = 100 + 20 + 1 and that the Method of Shewing what Fluxions are, by squaring them is entirely wrong. I suppose the 3 Mistakes he mention'd if they are such, may have been Slips of the Pen in transcribing. The other Piece, of the Several Species of Matter, he gave me his Opinion in these words, "It must necessarily have some further Meaning than the Language itself imports, otherwise I can by no means conceive the Service of it." —At the same time he express'd a high regard for you, as the ablest Thinker (so he express'd it) in the part of the World.[71]

John Rutherfurd, who was stationed in Albany at the time, was qualified to provide Colden with a critique of the work. Rutherfurd, the eldest son of Sir John Rutherfurd of Edgerton, Scotland, who was a friend of Colden's father, arrived in Albany to command an independent company in early 1742. Rutherfurd's position was that of a captain in charge of a military unit in Albany directed at limiting French-Canadian encroachments in the region. Within months of his arrival, he initiated correspondence with Colden indicating that: "I find my retirement here perfectly agreeable & for this reason, that 'tis compleat, dividing my time equally for Mathematicks, Philosphy, Politicks, &c without being interrupted in any Shape by Family cares of publick affairs as hitherto I have always been. . . ."[72]

Rutherfurd conveyed that he was knowledgeable about matters in physics, light and optics, mathematics, Cartesian and

Newtonian science, and the contributions of Boerhave in addition to appreciating the critical issues related to the Indians and the French.[73] All of their correspondence during Rutherfurd's presence in New York prior to his temporary return to Great Britain in 1748 pertained to military and Indian affairs, and Colden apparently did not share his treatise on gravitation with him. Rutherfurd resumed his command in New York, was promoted to major, and was killed in battle leading troops during a battle at Ticonderoga on July 8, 1758.

Colden did share his writings with Samuel Johnson (1696–1772). A more scientific and philosophical tone characterized their correspondence. Johnson was a native of Connecticut who was notable as a clergyman, educator, and philosopher. A graduate of the Collegiate School, which became Yale College and University, he initially became a Congregationalist minister but subsequently joined the Anglican Church. He was selected as the first president of King's College (the future Columbia University) in 1754. He was the chief proponent of the Irish philosopher George Berkeley in the colonies. As an "immaterialist" he argued against the absolute existence of matter and affirmed the merely relative existence of sensible things. The collegial epistolary dialogue between Colden, who has been regarded as the first of the American Materialists,[74] provides an early chapter in the history of American philosophy and establishes Colden as a notable metaphysician.

In 1745 Colden's *An Explication of the First Causes of Action in Matter; and of the Cause of Gravitation* (fig. 6) was published by James Parker in New York under the direction of James Alexander, whose proximity allowed him to oversee the project.[75] The forty-eight-page document was the first scientific treatise published in the colonies. About three hundred copies were printed, nine of which were sent to Peter Collinson in London to be distributed to knowledgeable individuals for their critiques.[76] One of these went to the Royal Society where "it is well Esteem'd & admir'd."[77] One

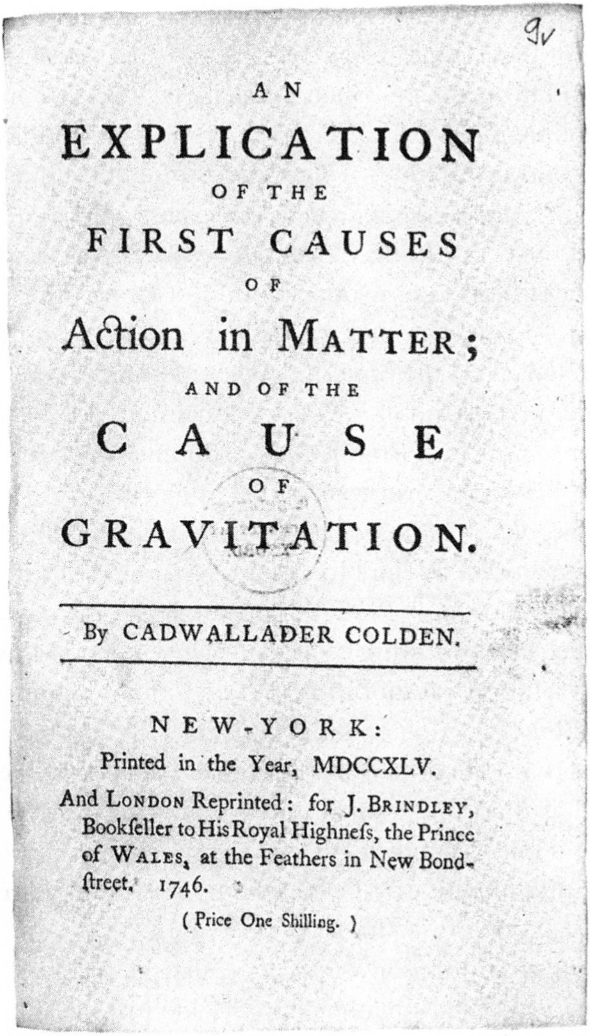

9v

AN

EXPLICATION

OF THE

FIRST CAUSES

OF

Action in MATTER;

AND OF THE

CAUSE

OF

GRAVITATION.

By CADWALLADER COLDEN.

NEW-YORK:

Printed in the Year, MDCCXLV.

And LONDON Reprinted: for J. BRINDLEY, Bookſeller to His Royal Highneſs, the Prince of WALES, at the Feathers in New Bond-ſtreet. 1746.

(Price One Shilling.)

Figure 6. Title page. Cadwallader Colden, *An Explication of the First Causes of Action in Matter, and the Cause of Gravitation,* printed by James Parker, New York, 1745. Quarto, 38 pages. The first scientific book printed in the British colonies in America.

of the recipients thought that the work was so sophisticated that it could not have come from America and that the shipwrecked papers of a European had fallen into Colden's possession.[78]

J. Brindley pirated the New York edition and published the work in London in 1746. A German translation appeared two years later. Almost immediately criticisms appeared. Samuel Johnson wrote from Stratford, Connecticut, that the rector of Yale said "he can't understand your Solution of Gravity; for two Balls in your *OEther*, will certainly be press'd as much by it on the Sides between them, as on the opposite Side, unless it has some Laws of Motion that we have never yet been acquainted with."[79] Collinson conveyed two criticisms from Britain including the statement, "Mr Colden is Mistaken in every part of his Conjectures."[80]

The designation of Colden as an "Early American Philosopher" is a byproduct of his attempt to expand Newtonian science. Much of Colden's philosophic thought appears in his correspondence with Samuel Johnson, which began in November 1743 with evidence that Johnson was supplying Colden with the complete works of Bishop Berkeley.[81] Colden's initial writing to Johnson concerned his own work on Fluxions. Johnson argued against Colden's supposition that there were an infinite number of parts in a finite quantity and Johnson indicated that they should be substituted for by small finite quantities.[82] Colden countered with an argument for his concept of infinite parts.[83]

In response to Johnson's indication that he was not qualified to understand Colden's mathematics, Colden wrote that, despite objections that had been made, he was as convinced of "it [his treatise] as if day light after sun is up & that it is more than an Hypothesis." He also expressed concern with being considered an atheist and dispelled that notion. In the same letter, the elements of Colden's personality that engendered many to dislike him are manifest in his criticism of Bishop Berkeley. He wrote of Berkeley that "he has made the greatest Collection in this & his other writings of both the Ancients and moderns that I have ever met with in anyone mans performance that he has the art of puzzling & confounding his readers in an elegant stile not common to such kind of writers & that he is a great abuser of the use of words as anyone of those that he blames most for that fault."[84]

The central disparity in the philosophical concepts of Johnson and Colden were summarized in a letter from Johnson to Colden.

> Whereas, therefore, you express your Definitions in these Terms, *And I take to be the Essential Differences between Matter & Spirit, that matter has it's[sic] Action regulated & determined by Efficient Causes, but Spirits by final Causes: I should have chose to express them thus, That matter has properly Speaking no Action, but in all it's [sic] Motions is merely passively acted & determined by Spirits which alone can be efficient Causes, whereas Spirits or Intelligent Beings are such as act from a principle of Consciousness & Design & and of Self Exertion & Self determination, under the influence or with a view at what we call final cause, i. e. some End which they aim at Accomplishing.*[85]

The draft of Colden's "First Principles of Morality, or of the Actions of Intelligent Beings" (n.d.), which represented a progression from physics to metaphysics, was the basis of what was at least a partial reconciliation of his own philosophical position with that of Johnson. Review of the draft allowed Johnson to ascribe their differences to a matter of semantics. Johnson had difficulty in accepting that *Action* could be attributed to *Matter* per se. Colden's statement that "The Actions [of the Body] are altered by efficient Causes *always* external to themselves" provided for an element of agreement with Johnson's position. As an Anglican minister, Johnson would have been satisfied because this allowed that the actions throughout nature that affect the senses and excite ideas are the actions of a Supreme Being or Spirit.[86]

The first recognition of Colden as an early American philosopher is ascribed to I. Woodbridge Riley, who credited Colden to be the earliest of the American materialists.[87] "Materialism" is a category in philosophy that maintains that matter constitutes the only reality and that everything, including thought and feeling, can be explained in terms of matter. Colden was considered by one author to be "the only important American materialist of the eighteenth century prior to the Revolution,"[88] and his philosophy provided "lines of investigation which were taken up by later materialists."[89] The most conspicuous early American materialist was Dr. Benjamin Rush.

Colden's "First Principles of Morality," which currently exists only as an unpublished draft, considers the human body as a machine with actions determined by man. He both derived from and, at the same time, was at variance with several predecessors, including Descartes, Spinoza, Hobbes, Leibniz, and Newton. According to Colden, all ideas that humans have of external entities come from action on the human senses. Colden considered an idea to be "the picture or representation of anything which we have received from our senses."[90] According to Colden, our knowledge of a substance is determined by that substance's action and the effects of that action. Thinking is a distinct kind of action. Matter is a sublimated force; mind is a spiritualized matter, which is not in opposition to other matter. Both possess the common denominator of a diffused, uniform elastic ether.

Matter is not regarded as passive. Rather, each type of matter possesses a force distinctive to itself. As such, Colden's "matter" is active and extended. But, the action of matter is determined by efficient causes external to itself.[91] When the action of matter is not determined by external causes and is indifferent to direction, then the intelligent being, using the ether's elasticity, directs action to suit its purpose.[92]

Unlike the belief of Samuel Johnson that all actions in nature that affect the senses are the actions of a Supreme Being or Spirit, Colden, who on several occasions declared that he was neither an atheist nor an agnostic, refused to recognize deistic control of actions and the senses. Colden was, at the same time, a deist, a materialist, and a Newtonian. Colden allowed the coexistence of an intelligent agent and unintelligent active matter. He claimed that the idea one has of a so-called Intelligent Being is related to its actions or operations just as are the ideas derived from the activity of material principles. Colden had to determine how material and intellectual "effects" were differentiated and how the innate activity of matter would not interfere with the activity of Intelligence.[93]

In contrast to Johnson's arguments as a philosophical Idealist (perceptions could only be attributed to a spiritual or mental cause), Colden opined that only a material agent could produce such perceptions.[94] For Colden, all beings were either agents or acting principles. "Nothing without action can produce anything." In Colden's materialism, there were two different kinds of beings. One included material agents that were determined by efficient causes and have neither perception nor consciousness. The other consisted of intelligent agents or beings that were conscious of their own actions and perceived actions of others that affect them. In Colden's terms, this represented differences between matter and spirit.[95]

Matter, acting as an agent with the capability of self-motion, possessed no innate order or system. It could not exist without a system in which it was included, which was referred to as the Intelligent Being. Even within this system, matter maintained its capability of self-activity. Colden argued against all activity being dependent on an "Almighty Spirit." He agreed with Johnson in his contempt for the Great Awakening religious movement, which had spread through the colonies. The movement that called for increased extreme emotionalism on the part of the congregation was inimical for Colden. He believed that religion ought to be based on reason "since there are no means to distinguish between true and false religion when we are not allowed to use our understanding in forming our judgment."[96]

Colden's *Principles of Morality* brings into focus the power of

the individual to determine his/her own actions without the inter-
ference of external forces. In the process, the individual considers
other "Intelligent Beings" in the same manner that the individual
regulates his or her other activities. Colden explained his use of
the terminology "Intelligent Beings" by distinguishing between its
general reference to "spirits" as contrasted with its use as "soul" or
"mind" when referring to human activity. Colden also emphasized
the distinction between intelligence and matter. The Intelligent
Being, which possesses neither shape nor dimensions, is dependent on the activity of matter, which has dimensions and is divis-
ible, for perception.

The mind, according to Colden, is a center of activity that func-
tions with a purpose, be it the avoidance of pain or the creation of
pleasure. Pleasure includes intellectual pleasure and the acquisition of knowledge. For Colden, morality is the "Art & Science of
living so as to be happy."[97] A balance should be achieved between
pleasures, and, in general, intellectual pleasures are more useful
and satisfying when compared with sensual pleasures. As a participant in the Enlightenment, in the stratification by Colden, pleasures are subservient to reason.

During the first half of the decade (between 1739 and 1748), an
increased amount of leisure time allowed for the most productive
period of Colden's intellectual pursuits. However, he continued
to serve the colony as a member of its Council in the administration of Lieutenant Governor Clarke, albeit with a reduced investment of his time. Colden and his political allies Lewis Morris and
James Alexander represented the minority opinion under Clarke
and, consequently, Colden infrequently attended meetings of the
Council. Colden's name is mentioned only once in William Smith,
Jr.'s *History of the Province of New-York*, in the chapter covering
Clarke's administration, and that relates to the controversy concerning Captain Campbell's proposal to settle land with Scotch
emigrants (see pp. 60–62).[98] Colden's published correspondence

for the period between 1738 and 1743 contains only one letter with any political implication, a brief but cordial note from Lieutenant Governor Clarke, apologizing for an inadvertent mistake by the clerk that might have been construed as injurious to Colden.[99]

The relative tranquility of the early part of the decade was offset by an all-consuming focus, during the second half of the decade, in which Colden fought to protect his reputation and maintain his political status. Relatively halcyon times precipitously transformed into a tempestuous period. On September 22, 1743, Governor George Clinton arrived in New York accompanied by his family. The early years of Clinton's administration were dominated by his attempt to augment the defense against those Indians who were allied with the French along the western and northern borders of the populated regions. In 1746, a newly elected Assembly increased the control of Chief Justice James Delancey, who was also a member of the Council, and opposed the governor's policies. The Assembly expressed enthusiasm for opposing the dangerous enemy but refused to advance money to underwrite the defense efforts.

In planning for a meeting with the Indians who were allied with the British colonials, the governor received little support from the Council. "He could prevail upon none of the Council to attend him, except Doctor Colden, Mr. Livingston, and Mr. Rutherford. From Mr. Delancey, by whom his measures had freely been directed, he was to expect no aid. They had quarreled in their cups, and set each other at defiance. The Governor then gave his confidence to Mr. Colden."[100]

After Colden and the governor arrived in Albany at the end on July, in anticipation of an increasing need for military preparation, Colden was able to secure for his son Cadwallader, Jr., the well-compensated position of commissary of musters.[101] At the opening of the August 1746 conference with the Indians in Albany, Governor Clinton was indisposed, and "left it to Mr. Colden to deliver a speech of his own drafting; and in his excuse for the absence of Mr. Clinton, he describes himself to the Indians as the next person in the administration, for Lieutenant Governor Clarke being gone to England, he was then the eldest member of the Council."[102]

In August, Colden formally opened the conference with the Indians who were allied with the New York colonials. According to the document that was printed to record the event, Colden stated: "His Excellency our Governor having been taken ill, and as yet not so well recovered as that he can safely come broad, has ordered me (being the next person to him in the Administration) to speak to you In his name, which I shall do in the same words which he designed to have spoke had he not been prevented by sickness."[103] The essence of the speech was an encouragement for the Indians to renew their covenant with the British, joining forces with the colonials by "taking up the Hatchet against our & your common Enemy's the French, & their Indians, who have in a very unmanly manner, by Sculking party's, muderer'd in Cold Blood, many of your Brethren, in this & the Province of Massachusetts Bay."[104]

On November 24, 1746, Governor Clinton issued a message to the Assembly in defense of his conduct at the Albany conference and his plan for operations against Canada. In the printed document, he included a preemptive defense of Colden's conduct related to the conference. He pointed out that the members of the Council deemed Colden to be an appropriate representative and that most other members declined attendance. He also stated that, if they perceived any inappropriateness in Colden's conduct, it should be excused. He stressed that Colden should not be maligned publicly because he was acting in accordance with the governor's orders. Clinton assertively concluded, "but there is something more than all this when I & he are considered in our present Stations as I am Governor of this Province & he is the person on whom the Administration devolves which may make the Tendency of these resolves deserve your most serious consideration."[105]

The crisis, which included a vitriolic personal attack by the Council on Colden, erupted on December 4th. When Colden entered the Council room he was confronted by Delancey with a printed copy of the account of the Albany treaty, which Colden admitted he had arranged for the printing. Colden was criticized for having indicated that members of the Council declined the governor's invitation to attend. Although this was true, it was construed to be an invidious attack on certain members of the Council. Four days later an account of the debate appeared in the New York periodical, *Post-boy*. Colden was presented as a vain individual who was focused on advancing himself, as evidenced by his referring to himself as the "next person to his Excellency in the administration."[106]

On December 16, Philip Livingston, James Delancey, Phillip Cortlandt, Dan Horsmanden, Joseph Murray, John Moore, and Stephen Bayard, submitted a *Representation to Clinton of seven members of the Council in reference to Colden's pamphlet of the Treaty with the Six Nations*. In an extensive and detailed document, the authors raised the issues of misrepresentation of facts regarding their lack of attendance at the Albany meeting and, also, Colden's desire to augment his own reputation and position at the expense of others. The seven councilmen summarized their criticism of Colden: "Mr Colden has Told the World in Print of his being the Next person to your Excellency in the Administration We shall Not Make Any Reflection on this Circumstance But Leave your Excellency to Consider, Whether it may Not be his Interest to Embroil your Exellencys Affairs And Distract your Administration, the Consequence of Which may be his getting the Reins of Government into his own hands, And here perhaps Your Excellency may find that, Which Was Intended As a Reflection Upon others One of those 'Artful and Designing Men' who *have* private Views."[107]

Three members of the governor's opposition and critics of Colden were also early members of the American Philosophical

Society. The first, James Delancey, whose brother, Peter, had married Colden's oldest daughter, Elizabeth, in 1737/38, was a Cambridge and Lincoln's Inn educated lawyer. He was a member of the Council of New York since 1729 and a justice of the colony's supreme court. As chief justice presiding over the trial of John Peter Zenger, Delancey held Zenger's attorneys in contempt. Delancey openly broke with Governor Clinton in 1744. Strengthened by his relationships with his old college friend Thomas Herring, Archbishop of Canterbury; his brother-in-law Admiral Sir Peter Warren; and his wife's cousin, Sir John Heathcote, a member of Parliament, Delancey was appointed lieutenant governor of New York in October 1747 in spite of Clinton's expressed desire that the position be awarded to Colden.

The second, Daniel Horsmanden, was also an English-educated lawyer who, on his arrival in New York, was befriended by Colden but later joined the Delancey faction in opposition to Clinton and Colden. On September 17, 1747, Clinton suspended Hormsmanden from the Council, and shortly thereafter removed him from the position of recorder and from the supreme court. He was restored to his positions in the 1750s. The third, Joseph Murray, was a London-educated, able, and respected lawyer.

In response to the personal attack, Colden dispatched a long letter of rebuttal to Governor Clinton, who was unswervingly supportive of Colden throughout a lengthy period of contention. Although Colden would not dismiss his personal characteristic of vanity, as he indicated it was manifested by many colonials, he explained that he presented himself at the Albany conference as the individual next to the governor in the administration in order to provide evidence of the governor's respect for his Indian allies.[108]

In the third week of March 1747, the Assembly met and the governor requested funding to supply presents to their Indian allies for an expedition to reduce the French fort at Crow Point and for the funding of one hundred scouts. The members of the

Assembly refused the request. Colden offered strong support for the governor and traced the greed of the opposition back to the administration of Governor Burnet. This led to Colden being referred to as "a person obnoxious to the house."[109]

In May, Colden, while in New York City, was made aware of a mutiny by the troops at Albany. This prompted correspondence with his wife at Coldengham, suggesting that she move the family that was in residence to one of her son's homes, because of the fear of reprisals.[110] Governor Clinton went to Albany without Colden to assuage the troops. In May 1747, Clinton wrote Thomas Pelham, Duke of Newcastle, who was in charge of colonial affairs in the ministry of Sir Robert Walpole, recommending that Colden be appointed lieutenant governor of New York.[111]

In 1747, a second edition of Colden's *The History of the Five Indian Nations* was published by Thomas Osborne in London. It included the material, ending with Denonnville's attack on the Senecas in 1689, that was included in the 1727 edition, to which was added a history of the Indians that extended to 1697 coincident with the signing of the Treaty of Ryswick. The map found in the 1747 edition is a reduced copy of Colden's original 1724 "Map of the Country of the Five Indian Nations." Within the 283-page publication, the first appended section following Part II is a reprint of Colden's *Papers relating to the Indian Trade* of New York, 1724. The second edition also includes Colden's *Papers Relating to the Indian Trade* as an appendix. In the *Papers*, Colden expressed concern with the mistreatment of the Indians by the colonists and the failure of the colonists and of Great Britain to appreciate the value of a positive relationship with the Indians in the process of expansion of the empire and trade.

Among Colden's papers, there is a draft in his handwriting of a *Continuation of Colden's History of the Five Indian Nations for the years 1707 through 1720.*[112] No manuscript has been found covering the years from 1697 to 1707. The extant manuscript chronicles a meeting between Lieutenant Governor Richard Ingoldesby and the Indians in July 1709, at which time the Indians were invited to join in an expedition against Canada. It also reports that in August 1710, Governor Robert Hunter met with the Five Nations at Albany and returned for another meeting a year later. Hunter is credited with maintaining a constant concern for his allies, the Five Nations, as evidenced by another with them in Albany in September 1719.[113]

The final year, 1748, of the decade in question opened with a disappointment for Colden. At the end of January, he was informed by Governor Clinton that Chief Justice Delancey had been appointed lieutenant governor by the Duke of Newcastle.[114] This occasioned a letter from Colden to the duke. Colden informed the duke that there was a faction in New York attempting to wrest control from the governor and as a consequence the Crown. The group, by authority of the Assembly, had made false attacks on the governor's character. In the letter the only mention made of Colden's own conflict with the opposition referred to the insinuation that he had participated in the Rebellion against the Crown in 1715, a point that he rebutted.[115]

Colden perceived Delancey to be his arch enemy. In a letter to the governor, Colden refers to him by position rather than name in characterizing the chief justice as "a person in this province of such insatiable Ambition and thirst after power . . . entirely directed by him as to curb & embroil your administration at pleasure & to have it in his power to do the same to any other administration. . . . His love of money On many occasions is as remarkable as his ambition & it is therefor most likely he will never be content with a half while he can hope to have the whole."[116]

The Assembly, which was convened in 1748, offered no support for the governor. Clinton became concerned that the heated arguments between Colden and Delancey might lead to his own recall to England or the termination of his appointment. Therefore he dismissed Colden from the Council and as a prime advisor, replacing him with Alexander.[117] Colden was reinstated in September, allowing a continuance of the heated argument between him and Delancey. That year, from his Ulster home, Colden issued "His Address to the Freeholders and Freemen of the Cities & Counties of the Province of New York by a Freeholder." He attacked the opposition's practice of making assertions without proof. He pointed out that their attempt to wrest authority from the king and parliament would engender resentment and adverse effects. Colden also attacked the personal interests and the desire of the wealthy members of the Council and Assembly who dominated the opposition to expand their estates.[118]

In late October, Colden first met Peter Kalm, who had been sent by Linnaeus to America to study the flora and fauna. Kalm wrote in his journal, "In the afternoon I called on Mr. C. Colden, who was then living in the town. He was minister in the government. He wielded great influence over the present governor, Clinton, so much that the latter almost always followed Mr. Colden's advice. On the other hand the majority of the people were very dissatisfied with Mr. Colden, whom they accused of all sorts of things."[119]

Despite his disappointment, Colden continued his activities in support of the governor. He petitioned for the appointment of his son John to the post of store keeper at Fort George. From April 24 through 26, Colden engaged in a conference with the Five Nations at Onondaga to retain their friendship.[120] Toward the end of the year, he received word from Franklin, who had put his printing business in the hands of David Hall, that Franklin had turned down the position of assemblyman in Philadelphia to allow for more time to read, study, experiment, and maintain his association with correspondents, particularly Colden.[121]

Chapter 5
CONTINUITY AND CHANGE

1749–1758

The decade, in which Cadwallader Colden lived the life of sexagenarian, was characterized by the continuance of a life spent mainly on his estate, with sporadic interjections of activities related to his roles as surveyor general and a member of the provincial Council. He remained a polarizing figure in the ever-expanding antipathy between the two competing political factions in New York. The one, which included Colden, sided with the governor and the Crown's control. The other, led by James Delancey and including the majority of the Assembly, favored more control by the colonists. Colden continued in his unswerving advocacy of Britain's imperialism and also in his attempts to gain personal recognition and appreciation in that regard. He used his long period of service without compensation as a platform for advancing the careers of his sons. The major change in the political arena was that the decade would become dominated by involvement of the province as a battleground during the early stages of the French and Indian War.

Colden's leisure time was continuously occupied by his attempts to gain recognition for what he perceived to be significant personal contributions to an understanding of the action of matter, the causes of gravitation, the principles of vital motion, and the transmission and reflection of light. By contrast, there was an apparent and expressed decrease in his interest in botany that was somewhat compensated for by the contributions of his daughter, whose expertise was a direct consequence of his deliberate direction. Although he had not practiced as a physician for the previous three decades, he maintained an interest in medicine as evidenced by his correspondence and the publication of articles on the subject.

At the onset of 1749, Colden wrote Governor Clinton in reference to the continuance of the opposition's publication of scandalous libels and their overt lack of respect for the king's authority as exercised by the governor.[1] Colden was comfortable in requesting that the governor appoint his son John clerk of the peace & of the common pleas for the city and county of Albany, as replacement for the recently deceased Philip Livingstone.[2] The affidavit for the appointment was executed in May with the stated provision that the profits, which accrue from the office, would be paid to Cadwallader.[3]

Governor William Shirley of Massachusetts was supportive of Governor Clinton and Colden, and served as a sympathetic sounding board for Colden's catharsis of his political concerns. In a long letter written to Shirley, Colden detailed the influence of Chief Justice Delancey, perhaps exceeding that of the governor. Colden indicated that the faction led by Delancey was desirous of a tyrannical government. Colden felt that he personally was in danger of a physical attack. Because the Assembly, controlled by Delancey's cohorts, blocked the financing required to protect the interests of the English colonists and allied Indians, Colden called upon Shirley to support Clinton and himself during Shirley's forthcoming trip to England.[4]

The Delancey-led faction relied on public opinion and the control of finances by the Assembly, which they dominated, to subvert the king's representative, the governor, and, consequently, the king's control. Colden's concern with political status in the Province of New York at that time was summarized in a letter to John Catherwood, the governor's secretary. According to Colden, the opposition continually acted to dissuade those who supported the kings prerogative and authority in theprovince. Colden wrote:

> I shall observe in general that the method they have taken to asperse Gov[rs] Character is such as the Greatest Villain would take to asperse the honestest man breathing & the only means that a villain can take. . . . It not only concerns the Ministry to discourage those Artifices which tend to destroy all Governm[t] & to bring every thing into confusion but likewise concerns every honest man who desires to enjoy his estate & liberty in safety. For if such principles be encouraged by success who can be safe. The greatest rogue the most abandon'd villain will be the greatest & most valued man where such attempts meet with success or publick approbation.[5]

Colden went on to point out that the governor had no power over the militia or the building and provisioning of the forts required to prevent incursions by the French Canadians and their allied Indians. The lack of financing had already precluded taking of the French fort at Crown Point on Lake Champlain and Fort Niagara on the Niagara River. Colden suggested that part of the solution was to have England directly appoint and salary the colonies' chief justices.

The year 1749 witnessed the publication the large "Map of Pensilvania, New-Jersey, New-York, and the Three Delaware Counties" by Lewis Evans (fig. 7) on which it is stated that "the greatest Part of New York Province is owing to the honourable Cadwallader Colden Esq." Coldengham is identified on the map and an inscription borrows from Benjamin Franklin's discovery for the statement "The Sea Clouds coming freightened with Electricity and inciting others less so, the Equilibrium is restored by Snaps of Lightning. . . ." The map is one of few to specifically locate Coldengham.

In 1750, John, the first Colden child to be born at Coldengham, died at age twenty-one. At age seventeen, he began running the farm when his parents were away. He served as the clerk of the city

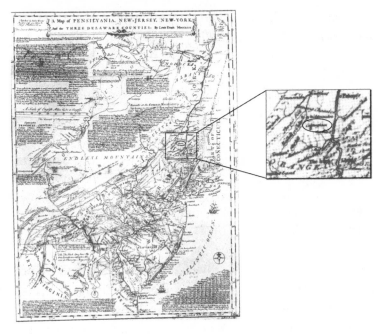

Figure 7. Lewis Evans, "A Map of Pensilvania, New-Jersey, New-York, and the Three Delaware Counties," 1749. Engraved (3rd state 1752), 64 x 48 cm. Courtesy Private Collector. The first map to depict the location of Coldengham. The material for the geography of New York and its boundaries was provided by Cadwallader Colden.

and county of Albany from March 1749. Cadwallader was in New York City when he learned of his son's death. He had insufficient funds with him to pay the legacy and funeral expenses and he sent home for forty pounds.[6]

Colden, after serving over thirty years as surveyor general for the province, informed Governor Clinton that age had become a limiting factor. Colden requested that his son Alexander be appointed as his replacement. Colden expressed concern related to the "malice" against "myself tho' it may be restrain'd yet never ceases & only waits for a proper opportunity to exert itself."[7] In 1737, Alexander had been appointed ranger of Ulster County, where he operated a country store. In 1751, Alexander was appointed joint surveyor general of New York and became acting surveyor general when his father became acting governor in 1761. He was also post master of New York until his death in 1774.

Colden's continuous concern for his children's future is manifest in a 1755 letter to Peter Collinson.

I am under concern that all the care and trouble which I have taken should turn out so little advantage of my children & so very far short of what I might have done had I turn my thoughts as others commonly do to the advanceing my private fortune without any regard to the public weal. I now have seven children alive grown up to the state of men & woemen and twenty grand children. My children I am confident are allowed by all who know them to be deserving & my grand children promise as well as any children in the Country. . . ."[8]

Throughout the remainder of Governor Clinton's tenure political animosities and polarization between his supporters and the faction led by Chief Justice Delancey continued. There was a move to suspend Delancey's appointment as lieutenant governor and appoint another. It was deemed more tactful to apply to the king and have him personally recall the commission.[9] John Catherwood, secretary to Governor Clinton, also endorsed the removal of Delancey from the post of lieutenant governor.[10]

Delancey's influence persisted. When the governor's spokesmen addressed the Assembly made up of Delancey's cronies and relatives, they deliberately articulated messages that "were least calculated to kindle the party fires which Mr. Colden's incautious, luxuriant compositions and high principles had so often exasperated, to the advancement of the popularity of the person he meant to pull down."[11] Clinton, who would be recalled and become a member of Parliament, continued to support Colden as evidenced by the last letter to Colden just six months before transferring the governorship to Sir Danvers Osborn.[12]

During this period, in appreciation of his aging, Colden evidenced concern with his finances. He desired that a salary be attached to the office of surveyor general, and that the salary come from the king in view of the attitude of the Assembly.[13] Colden also addressed his two main correspondents in England requesting that they act on his behalf regarding the recently vacated position of deputy post master general of America. To Collinson, Colden wrote that the salary of 300 pounds sterling was particularly attractive because it required little effort and would therefore allow him to continue to pursue his intellectual interests. Colden indicated that he was particularly deserving, because, unlike the two previous predecessors who lived in Virginia, his location in New York placed him in the center of business. In addition, his long-term public service unaccompanied by any allowance from the Crown merited consideration.[14]

At the same time, Colden wrote John Mitchell soliciting his assistance in obtaining the position of deputy post master general. Colden, once again stressed that he had served the government for about thirty years without salary, and confessed that "I never had any talent at getting or saving money tho' I never was expensive but I have had a large family to support & I wish to be usefull to them before I leave them."[15] This was an embarrassment for Mitchell, who had applied for the post himself.[16] Colden was informed of this by John Rutherfurd, who wrote that he thought that Mitchell would be appointed.[17] After a long period of consideration, on August 10, 1753, Benjamin Franklin received the appointment.

In May 1753, a letter from George Montagu Dunk, the Second Earl of Halifax, who was president of the Board of Trade from 1748–1761, written in response to a letter from Colden, added to Colden's disappointment. Although the earl informed Colden that there was no reason to suppose that there was any disapprobation of Colden's character or performance, he affirmed the appointment of Delancey as lieutenant governor. He also indicated that it was not appropriate to remove Delancey from his seat on the Council. The earl added that the Crown could not provide a salary for the position of surveyor general. He went on to report that Sir Danvers Osborn would soon assume the governorship of the province of New York, and concluded with "My earnest wish is that even the Remembrance of former animosities would no longer remain, and that the only Contention for the future may be who shall most effectually promote the welfare Peace and Tranquillity of the Province."[18]

On October 7, 1753, Osborn arrived in New York City to take up his post as governor. The last act of Clinton's administration was the delivery to Delancey of his commission to be lieutenant governor. This was performed at a meeting of the Council immediately after presenting the seal of office to Osborn. On October 11, the new governor convened the Council. The next morning between seven and eight, he was found dead, hanging in the garden of the home where he had been staying.[19]

As lieutenant governor, Delancey assumed control of the administration, a situation that would persist for two years. Regaled with the adulation of his faction, he convened the strongly supportive Assembly, which extolled his abilities and virtues. This was followed by an overt focus on what they defined as the malicious "mal-administration" of Governor Clinton. The Assembly listed nine specific instances of Clinton's activities that generated deep dissatisfaction. Meanwhile, Colden had retired to his country estate, a disheartened man who had witnessed passage of a commission of lieutenant governor, which he had desired, to his enemy, Delancey. His plan to neutralize the enemy had failed.[20]

Sir Charles Hardy, the recently appointed governor of New York arrived in New York City on September 2, 1755. As a part of Hardy's commission, Delancey was added to the Council. Although Hardy had been named governor of Newfoundland in

1744, he never visited the island in that capacity. He was a naval officer with no tested administrative experience. He, therefore, relied heavily on Delancey. Correspondence between Colden and Hardy focused on the protection of the frontiers and the building of blockhouses to abort attacks.[21]

In 1756, the incursions by hostile Indians in Ulster and Orange Counties evoked an article in the *Gazette* censuring the Assembly. Initially, Colden was suspected of being the author, but the article was traced to a local Episcopal clergyman. A bill for raising and funding a militia was proposed. It was opposed by Colden, who deemed it insufficient. The Council sided with Colden, and the bill was consequently modified and passed.[22] James Alexander, Colden's closest friend, exposed himself to inclement weather to attend the vote. He became ill and died shortly thereafter. On July 2, 1757, Hardy ended his governorship and hoisted his flag as rear admiral of the Blue in support of an expedition against Louisbourg. The administration of the province of New York reverted to Delancey.

The decade that extended from 1749 to 1758, for New Yorkers, was dominated by concern related to aggression and aggrandizement by the French Canadians and their Indian allies. The earlier years of that period were characterized by a sense of anticipation and a realization of the need to take protective measures. During the latter years, the soil of the province of New York was bloodied as the major site of what came to be known as the French and Indian War.

From the early part of the seventeenth century both England and France had staked claims on the North American continent. In 1713, as part of the Treaty of Utrecht, France ceded to Great Britain claims to the Hudson's Bay Company in Rupert's Land, Newfoundland, and Acadia. France was also to recognize British control over the Iroquois while trade with the more western Indians was open to traders of both nations. France retained control of Ile-

Saint Jean (Prince Edward Island) and Ile Royale (Cape Breton Island). In 1748, the Treaty of Aix-la-Chapelle was confirmed by the Treaty of Utrecht.

The French had a long history of establishing forts to protect their commercial interests. In 1672, they built a fort on the north shore of the east entrance of Lake Ontario. A year later, they built a fort at Michilimackinac, where Lakes Huron, Michigan, and Superior come together. In 1684, a fort was erected at Niagara on the strait between Lakes Erie and Ontario. In 1732, they built a modern fort at Louisbourg on Cape Breton, subsequently built forts in Acadia and at Crown Point on Lake Champlain.

The British countered with construction of Fort Oswego on the southeastern shore of Lake Ontario in 1727 and the establishment of Halifax to rival Louisbourg in 1749. British claims and large land grants were extended into the Ohio Valley. As a consequence, in 1749 troops were sent forth from Montreal to the shores of the Allegheny and Ohio Rivers demanding that the British retreat to the eastern slopes of the Appalachian Mountains.

In a long letter written in August 1751, Colden summarized the state of Indian affairs for Governor Clinton.[23] Colden detailed the events that had taken place since Clinton's initial engagement with the leadership of the Six Nations. The commissioners for Indian affairs had become totally ineffective and the conduct of Indian affairs was delegated to the leadership of Colonel William Johnson, who had been adopted as a member of the Iroquois and was highly regarded by them. Johnson resigned his governmental position because he had received insufficient funds to gain influence and was required to expend his own monies. When skirmishes with Indians allied with the French broke out, Johnson advanced his own funds to supply the garrison at Fort Oswego. The Assembly refused to advance funds or reimburse Johnson. The Indians allied with the British felt cheated by the British traders.

In the same letter, Colden suggested that the provincials build a fort on the northeastern shore of Lake Ontario near the origin of the St. Lawrence River to counterbalance Fort Frontenac, which the French had recently built. He indicated that measures should be taken against the French fort at Crown Point in order to stop trade between Albany and Canada. He also championed the construction of a fort between Albany and Wood Creek on the route from Albany to Canada.

The onset of the French and Indian War was specifically related to the interests of the Virginia colony in the Ohio Valley. When Lieutenant Governor Robert Dinwiddie of Virginia learned that the French had recently built two forts near the south shore of Lake Erie and had stationed 1,500 regular troops in the area, on October 31, 1753, he dispatched George Washington, a twenty-one-year-old colonel in the Virginia militia, on a mission to insist that the French depart. During his journey of more than 500 miles, Washington surveyed the fork of the Ohio River, where the Allegheny River and Monongahela River joined, and suggested that it provided the optimal site for a fort in the region.

On February 17, 1754, work was begun on a redoubt, which was to become Fort Prince George, in honor of the heir to the British throne. On April 18, Captain Pierre de Contrecoeur, in command of 500 troops, took possession of the barely begun building. The French completed the structure and named it Fort Duquesne. At the same time Washington led troops from Virginia to the area where he learned of the surrender. Washington encamped at Great Meadows, about sixty-five miles southwest of the forks of the Ohio. On May 28, he attacked a small group of French troops, that was also camped in the area. The French later maintained that Washington's action initiated the war.[24] Anticipating reprisals, Washington erected a stockade at Great Meadows and named it Fort Necessity. On July 3, seven hundred French troops and over 350 Indians attacked the fort, and four hours later, Washington surrendered. He and his small contingent were allowed to return home.

At the same time that Washington was active in the Ohio Valley, diplomatic activity occurred in the northeastern colonies. Prior to opening of a proposed convention, Colden wrote Franklin his "Remarks on short hints to a Scheme for uniting the Northern Colonies."[25] He questioned whether, when the colonies were united for defense, it should be accomplished by an act of Parliament or by the assemblies. He also queried whether the designated governor general would have legislative authority and suggested that the grand council should be elected for a long tenure.

A convention for the adoption of a Plan of Union of the Colonies met at the courthouse in Albany on July 10, 1754. Representatives of all of the colonies, with the exception of Georgia and Delaware, attended. James Delancey, as the only governor in attendance, presided. Franklin reported a draft of a proposal that would establish a president general and a grand council of forty-eight members from the eleven colonies represented.[26] Every representative at the convention consented to the plan with the exception of Delancey, who did not express opposition.[27] In spite of Franklin's historic cartoon "Join or Die," the first political cartoon published in America (fig. 8), the convention failed to accomplish any of its goals.

In February 1755, British Major General Edward Braddock arrived in Virginia with two regiments and presented plans for a three-pronged attack to contain the French. The Massachusetts force was to refurbish Fort Oswego and then capture Fort Niagara. Colonel William Johnson, with New York troops and Iroquois allies, were to capture Fort Frederick at Crown Point on Lake Champlain. Braddock would achieve the surrender of Fort Duquesne and gain control of the Ohio Valley. Unrelated to Braddock's plan, in June, the Massachusetts militia, with naval support, took possession of Fort Beausejour in French Acadia and renamed the area Nova Scotia.

Shortly thereafter, Braddock embarked on his assault on Fort Duquesne. On July 8 the British were routed. Braddock was mortally wounded, and 907 of 1,459 British troops were

Figure 8. "Join or Die" cartoon by Benjamin Franklin. First published in the Philadelphia *Gazette* May 9, 1754. The first political cartoon published in America.

killed or wounded.[28] Washington, who participated as a volunteer without rank or pay, had two horses shot from under him. Although several bullets pierced his clothing, he was not wounded.[29] Despite knowledge of that defeat, the Massachusetts troops proceeded to Fort Oswego and secured the post but General Shirley elected to defer an attack on Fort Niagara.

New York occupied center stage in the conflict for two years. History had sensitized the citizens. On November 28, 1745, a party of French and Indians destroyed the community of over one hundred individuals at Saratoga; the fort was later abandoned in 1747. In 1748, skirmishes occurred in the vicinity of Schenectady where several cabins were destroyed. In 1755, William Johnson, an Irish immigrant who became the most influential individual in maintaining the alliance between the New York colonials and the

Iroquois, was assigned the leadership of a proposed attack on Fort Frederick at Crown Point.

In July, as the troops proceeded toward the southern shore of Lac Saint Sacrament, they constructed a fort, which would ultimately be named Fort Edward. When Johnson's contingent reached the lake, he renamed it Lake George to honor the king, and built Fort William Henry to protect the area. On September 8, the battle that pitted Johnson's troops against a French force led by Commander-in-Chief Marshall Dieskau resulted in a stirring victory for the British and included the capture of the French commander.

On March 18, 1756, Great Britain formally declared war on France, and France reciprocated the next day. A string of forts were built between Albany and Lake Ontario. Fort Williams was constructed on the shore of the Mohawk River near Wood Creek; Fort Bull was built four miles to the west; a blockhouse erected at the east end of Lake Oneida; Fort Herkimer was built at German Flats. The fort at Oswego was reinforced by the Massachusetts militia. The French destroyed Fort Bull, and led by the new Commander-in-Chief Louis-Joseph de Montcalm, captured Fort Oswego on August 14, taking 1,600 prisoners.[30] Toward the end of that year, Colden reported that about sixteen miles from Coldengham Indians burned several homes and murdered the inhabitants.[31]

In March 1757, the British repulsed four French attacks on Fort William Henry. Five months later, the French, led by Montcalm, forced the fort to capitulate. In spite of Montcalm's attempt to control his Indian allies, they went on a rampage wildly assaulting and killing the occupants of the fort who had surrendered. At the time the battle was about to take place, Cadwallader Colden received a detailed letter from his son Alexander in Albany. Alexander informed his father of the investment of Fort Edward by the French and the large number of French troops that had taken up their battle positions at Fort William Henry.[32] Subsequent letters written from son to father over the ensuing weeks detailed the travesty that occurred at Fort William Henry.[33]

In September of that year, Colden informed Delancey that, since the frontiers of Ulster and Orange Counties were enforced with the militia after the last incursion by Indians allied with the French, the local farmers had returned to their homes.[34] Two months later, he indicated to the lieutenant governor that he was proceeding to erect a series of blockhouses, each to be manned by twenty men, to provide defense in the vicinity of Coldengham. In that letter Colden reported that he was moving with his wife and daughters to Flushing on Long Island.[35] Shortly after he moved, "a large party of French & Indians Surprised Burnetsfield, a fine Village of Germans on the Mohawk river. . . . The Village is burnt & destroyed, about 12 persons killed, and above 200 carried away prisoners."[36]

The year 1758 marked the beginning of the turn in the tide of battle to the advantage of the British. William Pitt the Elder, who had initially been appointed secretary of state on December 4, 1756, and dismissed four months later, was reappointed on June 29, 1757. He intensified British activity in North America, increasing the supplies and allocation of troops. On July 26, after forty-nine days of bombardment, the French fort at Louisbourg on Cape Breton capitulated. The two other British goals for that year were the capture of Ticonderoga and Fort Duquesne.

On July 8, the British attacked Fort Carillon at Ticonderoga, but suffered a major defeat. Colden provided his constant correspondent, Collinson, with a detailed account of the event. In his letter, he indicated that his close friend Major John Rutherfurd of the Royal Americans lost his life during battle.[37] To compensate for that defeat, Fort Stanwix was built on the shore of the Mohawk River near Schenectady, and Fort Frontenac on Lake Ontario was captured on August 27. Fort Frontenac had provided the main source of supplies for both Forts Niagara and Duquesne.

In the course of the defeat of the French at Fort Frontenac, the entire French fleet on Lake Ontario was captured. In September the battle for Fort Duquesne was begun under the leadership of Brigadier General Forbes. On November 24, the French dismantled, burned, and abandoned the fort. Two days later, the fortress was renamed Fort Pitt.

During the decade Colden remained peripheral to the major events of the ongoing war, and he participated infrequently in the deliberations and declarations of the provincial Council. It was a time during which hours of leisure could be dedicated to his persistent reflections on topics of medicine, the history of the Five Nations, the laws of physics and optics, and botany.

In 1751, Colden published in *Gentlemen's Magazine* an article on the value of pokeweed (*Phytolacca*, probably *P. decandra*) as a cure for cancer.[38] Colden indicated that the successful use of pokeweed had been reported by Doctor Samuel Johnson of Stratford, Connecticut. Colden, however, wrote that there was no rational basis for its efficacy and that he had no knowledge of a certain cure. Colden provided a botanical description of the plant and described how the corrosive juice of the plant was applied to the cancerous growth or ulcer. A year later Colden wrote Franklin, "No doubt you have seen the Cure of Cancer by the Poke weed published in the Gent[ms] Magazine I have lately had a confirmation of this by a Cancer last year cured in a Womans breast I have no doubt it will generally make a perfect cure of a genuine Cancer from many Accounts."[39] It is interesting that pokeweed nitrogen is currently used to provoke B lymphocyte proliferation in culture, suggesting an immunologic influence.

The same year, Colden wrote the New York printer James Parker suggesting the publication of a cure for hydrophobia caused by the bite of a dog. Colden referred to a report in newspapers in England by Doctor Mead. Mead reported that the therapy never failed if was applied after the bite and before the manifestations of hydrophobia (rabies) began. Treatment consisted of blood-letting and the use of medicine extracted from moss.[40] In 1753, Colden's letter to Doctor John Fothergill of London, "Concerning the Throat–Distemper" was published in the London *Medical Observations and Inquiries*.[41]

Interest in Colden's *History of the Five Indian Nations* rapidly waned. Whereas all 500 copies of the first edition printed by William Bradford in New York were sold,[42] the 1747 London edition was less successful. The publisher, Thomas Osborne, initially was encouraging. A year after the publication, he wrote Colden, "The Book was received in the World with the greatest Reputation; But I find in most Books after there has been a Run of about two or three hundred, that it drops off but slowly, which is the Case of this, for I have Actually by me near 500 Books."[43] Within two years of writing that letter, Osborne sold the remainder of the edition and his rights in it to another publisher.

In June 1751, Osborne indicated to Colden, "S[r] I have Receiv'd the favour of both yours & Should have Answer'd the first before but that was upon so melancholy a Subject that I deferr'd writing as you will find hereafter Its True that I did inform you that the Indian History was well receiv'd but for what Reason I cannot tell the Sale of it fell off before I sold one Quarter and the Impression and the Demand has been So very Smal ever Since That I was Glad to dispose of them at any Rate and what I had remaining upon my hands, I sold for Twelve Pence a Book, so that I am a Loser by that undertaking at least Thirty pounds Therefore I cannot give Encouragement to continue it on I shall be proud of Serving you with any Thing that I have but am determined for the future to Trade for nothing but ready money by which means I can afford to Sell cheaper than another."[44]

In 1750, another second Edition was printed for John Whiston, at Mr. Boyle's Head, and Lockyer Davis at Lord Beacon's Head, both in Fleet-street, and John Ward opposite the Royal

Exchange. In 1755, a third Edition was printed for Lockyer Davis, J. Wren in Salisbury-court, and J. Ward in Cornhill, opposite the Royal-Exchange.[45] Much of Colden's leisure time was consumed by his defense of his 1745 forty-eight page publication on action in matter and gravitation. In 1750, he wrote to Dr. Betts in London indicating that he had received little response to the notions expressed in the work, which suggested that it was regarded to be of little importance. Colden went on in that letter to affirm that, nevertheless, he had not been dissuaded from continuing his reflections. These included the application of his principles to the motion of the planets and the regulation of their course in their orbits. Colden, with a modicum of reserve, pointed out that he had provided an argument that Newton's theory of planetary motion was imperfect. Colden's hubris found expression in his assessment of his contributions. "I am fully persuaded that they will at last prevail & tho they may not suite the present taste of learning they will some how or other be embraced perhaps when the author is dead & forgot."[46]

Peter Collinson would arrange for the 1751 publication of a revised and enlarged (215-page) English edition under a new title, *The Principles of Action in Matter, the Gravitation of Bodies and the Motion of the Planets, explained from those Principles.* Abstracts appeared in *Monthly Review, Gentlemen's Magazine,* and *London Magazine.* [47] In the work, Colden pointed out that Newton had not defined the cause of gravitation or the cause of motion of the planets. Colden stated, "In this tract, the author presumes to think, that he has discovered the cause of this apparent attraction, and from which all the phenomena in gravitation evidently follow, as necessary consequences: and that he has likewise discovered an error, which has slipped from the sagacious Sir Isaac, by his not knowing the cause of this apparent attraction."[48] This would result in a continuance of adverse criticism during subsequent periods of consideration.

Perhaps the most devastating comments were those made

by Professor Euler of Berlin that were forwarded to Colden by Collinson.[49] Leonhard Euler was considered to be the preeminent mathematician of the eighteenth century and one of the greatest of all mathematicians. He has been honored with commemorative stamps by the Soviet Union and the German Republic, both venues of his work. Euler wrote: "The Book contains many Ingenious Reflections upon that Subject for a Man that has not entirely devoted Himself to a Study of it. . . . This shows but little knowledge of the principles of Motion & entirely disqualifies the author from Establishing the True Forces requisite to the Motion of the Planets. . . . Besides his explication on the Elasticity of the Ether is so ill imagined, that it is absolutely contrary to the first principles of Hydrostaticks. What an absurdity it is. . . ." A year later, Colden wrote to Franklin, "Mr Collinson sent me some remarks made on it by Professor Euler of Berlin. He writes much like a Pedant highly conceited of himself."[50]

Abraham Gotthelf Kastner, professor of mathematics at Leipzig, who translated the 1751 edition into German, was also critical of the work and indicated that Colden was deficient in mathematical understanding.[51] Kastner condescendingly added, "It would be something remarkable, if we could obtain from America, the solution of difficulties in physics, which have seemed insurmountable to the greatest geniuses of Europe, & if that, what was incomprehensible to a Newton should now be cleared up, by a countryman from the New World."[52]

The criticism emanating from authorities failed to dissuade Colden. On November 19, 1754, Colden sent Collinson a revised copy of the *Principles* with the accompanying message: "I have been more at leisure these twelve months passed than I have been for several years before I have taken this Opportunity to re-examine the Principles of Action in matter if I could not free them from just objections with a view to abandon those Principles. . . . After the greatest attention & care I am Capable I still remain persuaded of the truth of them & that they may be of use in every part of Physics."[53]

Colden amended the work, adding the observations of astronomers and also Newton's observations on light and colors. Colden suggested that his contribution might be of assistance in resolving the problem of astronomically measuring longitude at sea, for which a grand prize had recently been announced. Colden placed himself in the company of Descartes, who supplanted the authority of Aristotle and Newton, who affected Descartes similarly.[54]

The last person to comment on Colden's work was Doctor John Bevis, who was a contributor of articles on astronomy and meteorology to *Gentleman's Magazine* and who responded to Collinson's solicitation. In 1755, Bevis stated that Colden's principles were in opposition to the established laws of mechanics and that Colden incorrectly separated self-motion from direction.[55]

Ultimately, the manuscript of the revision was sent, in 1763, by Colden to Doctor Robert Whytt, professor of physiology and pathology at Edinburgh. He wrote Colden that if publication were not achieved, the manuscript would be submitted as a present and "that on the cover, mention should be made of these papers having been written by you, & made a present of, to y[e] University of Edin[r] where you had your first Education; as you imagine that they may contain the true principles of Physics and one day become usefull."[56] Colden agreed and asked Whytt if it "will not be assuming too much to myself" to make the transfer.[57]

During the decade between 1749 and 1758, the prolific correspondence between Colden and Franklin continued, and over two dozen letters passed between them. Colden wrote Franklin concerning the "Proposals relating to the Education of Youth in Pensylvania," which he assumed were written by Franklin. Colden suggested that the rector or principal overseer of the education should have a salary, which was dependent on fees from the scholars. He was particularly pleased that agriculture had been included as one of the sciences and thought that the college should be distant from the distractions of city life. Colden did not think that Latin and Greek should be required, and indicated that the English language, both prose and poetry, should be stressed.[58]

In 1750, Franklin sent Colden observations and experiments on electricity and a new hypothesis on the cause and effects of lightning.[59] Colden praised Franklin's experiments, but indicated that he was unable to formulate a cause for electricity, which he ascribed to "most subtile elastic fluid."[60] In response to Franklin's jocular comment that "I am much in the *Dark* about *Light*,"[61] Colden provided Franklin with an explanation of his own theory.[62] In October 1752, Colden wrote Franklin that he read in the newspapers about the account of the "Electrical Kite."[63] A year later, Franklin informed Colden that he had altered his theory regarding lightning; the clouds are "electrified negatively & the Earth positively . . . But as to the Methods propos'd for *Practice*, to guard against the Mischiefs of Lightning, they remain the same."[64]

David Colden, Cadwallader's youngest son, developed an interest in the subject of electricity. He conducted his own experiments and, in 1753, he dispatched a long and detailed letter to Abbé Nollet in response to Nollet's letters to Franklin. Nollet was a French priest who became the first professor of experimental physics at the University of Paris. Nollet had offered arguments opposing Franklin's theory of electricity, and David's correspondence was an attempt to reconcile the differences.[65] In 1757, while Franklin was in England, Cadwallader Colden wrote that he was pleased to have received a copy of Franklin's experiments on electricity. Colden confessed his personal ignorance and stated, "In the time I have been allowed amidst perpetual avocations to think on your experiments they seem to me to lead more directly to the cause than any set of experiments which I have seen."[66]

The Colden-Franklin correspondence of 1753 and 1754 contains a disagreement about the phenomenon of water spouts.

Franklin was of the opinion that water spouts were the result of an ascending of the sea water due to whirlwinds. Colden initially wrote Franklin that, from his own observations, he concluded that Franklin's explanation was false. The creation of the spout, according to Colden could not have been the result of sucking water from the sea. Rather, Colden suggested that the spout was caused by the violent stream of wind that created a hollow on the surface of the water and raised the water in a circular uneven ring around the hollow.[67] Colden later wrote Franklin, "I long to see your explication of Water spouts but I must tell you beforehand that it will not be easy for you to convince me that the principle phenomena were not occasioned by a stream of Wind issuing with great force. My eyes & ears both concurring to give me this sentiment."[68] Franklin was unmoved by Colden's objection and the subject was disputed by members of the Royal Society. Eventually the secretary recorded, "It seems yet undetermined which of the two opinions is best supported."[69] Colden later proved to be correct.

Botany remained the one realm in which Cadwallader Colden generated no argument, no significant disagreement, no polarization, and maintained a position of high regard. At the beginning of the decade in question, in February 1749, Colden wrote Linnaeus that political commitments of the previous three years precluded his "Botanical amusements."[70] Peter Kalm, who had been appointed by the Royal Swedish Academy of Science to travel to America to gather plants and seeds and make observations of the region, arrived in Philadelphia, subsequently visited Coldengham, and later requested a biography from Colden to be included in a proposed *Biographia Botanicorum*.[71]

In 1750, Colden confessed in his correspondence that he was aging. "I am now in my Grand Climacteric both my imagination & mind begin to flag & my health will not permit much application of mind at any time."[72] But, this did not prevent him from complying with Kalm's request for a personal biography. The biography that Colden submitted was factual and unembellished and he claimed no expertise in the science of botany.[73]

Toward the end of 1754, a letter from Alexander Garden introduced him as part of the coterie of Colden's correspondents, who shared an interest in botany.[74]

ALEXANDER GARDEN

Alexander Garden, who was forty-two years younger than Colden, shared several points of similarity with Colden in addition to an avid interest in botany. Garden was born in January 1730 in Birse, Aberdeenshire, Scotland, the son of a clergyman in the Church of Scotland. From 1743 to 1746, he was apprenticed to James Gordon, professor of medicine at Marischal College, Aberdeen, where Garden studied. After he was unable to obtain an appoint as a surgeon's second mate in the British navy, he returned as an apprentice to Gordon. From 1748 to 1750 he served as a surgeon's first mate aboard three ships. In 1750, he continued his medical studies at the University of Edinburgh, where his exposure to Charles Alston, the King's Botanist and Keeper of the Garden at Holyrood, stimulated his lifelong passion for botany. Garden received an MD degree from Marischal in 1752. Two years later he arrived in Prince William Parish, near Charles Town, South Carolina, to join the practice of William Rose.[75]

Garden immediately began his correspondence with the leading botanists from England and Europe, initiated his studies of the flora in his vicinity, and extended those studies into Florida. In 1754, he traveled north, specifically, to meet Benjamin Franklin, John Bartram, and, subsequently, Cadwallader Colden. During his visit at Coldengham he gained an appreciation of Colden's daughter Jane's expertise in botany. Jane Colden was only five years older than Garden and when her father was occupied she served as hostess.[76] Garden wrote to his friend John Ellis, the author of *Agriculture Improved* and *The Farmer's Instructor,* "Not only the doctor himself is a great botanist, but his lovely daughter is a great master of the Linnaean method, and cultivates it with great assiduity."[77] It was the beginning of an extended period of communication between Jane and Alexander and the occasional exchange of seeds and plants. During Garden's stay at Coldengham, John Bartram unexpectedly arrived.[78]

In 1755, Garden returned to Charles Town where he developed a large medical practice. That year he accompanied South Carolina's governor, James Glen, on an expedition to the Cherokee territory in the Blue Ridge Mountains. In January he sent the Coldens seeds of *Magnolia, Guatemala Indigo, Button snakeroot* (a powerful diaphoretic), *Catalpa, Dahoon Holly* (an Evergreen), *Palmetto,* and *Renialemia.* The accompanying letter informed Colden that the Montagu house had been purchased for the repository of Sir Hans Sloane's collection and the Cotton Library and Harleian manuscripts. This was the genesis of The British Museum. The letter also mentioned Doctor James Lind's classic treatise on Scurvy.[79] The same year, Garden first wrote Linnaeus; this was the beginning of an extensive and long-term correspondence. In 1755, Garden was elected as the first corresponding member of the London Society of Arts and also the Premium Society, which was founded in London that year for granting premiums in Britain and the colonies for the encouragement of commerce, manufacturing, and agriculture. Colden was made a member on Garden's recommendation.[80]

Garden made no landmark discoveries, but was particularly notable for his ability to classify plants. In several disputes with Linnaeus, Garden proved to be correct.[81] Sometime in the 1760s, Garden sent Linnaeus a dissertation on the Carolina Siren, an amphibious mud iguana, which Linnaeus said was not only a new genus but a new class or order (*Siren lacertian*).[82] Garden was recognized for his descriptions of the flora and fauna of America by election to the Philosophical Society of Edinbugh, the Royal Society of Uppsala, and the Royal Society of London. In 1768, he was elected a corresponding member of the American Society for Promoting and Propagating Useful Knowledge, the Philadelphia Medical Society, and the American Philosophical Society.[83]

In 1765, the opposition to the Stamp Act in Charleston led Garden to proclaim in a letter, "The die is thrown for the sovereignty of America!"[84] Throughout the American Revolution, Garden continued to practice medicine in Charles Town but his loyalty to the British crown was manifest. Consequently, in 1782, his property was confiscated and he was formally banished. His son, Alexander, rose to the rank of major and aide-de-camp to General Nathanael Greene in the American Army during the American Revolution. The abandoned Garden plantation was taken over by the son. Alexander senior died in 1791 in London after a long illness.

A proposal to attach Garden's name to a plant was first made by Jane Colden. James Britten, in his paper "Jane Colden and the Flora of New York" wrote, "The plant (*Hypericum virginicum*) . . . had been sent her by Alexander Garden, who found it in New York in 1754; in return, Miss Colden sent him the description of the same plant, which she had discovered the previous summer, and 'using the privilege of a first discoverer she was pleased to call this new plant *Gardenia*, in compliment to Dr. Garden."[85] Unfortunately, the plant in question turned out not to be new, and Garden's name was not attached.[86] But, in 1760, John Ellis named the genus *Gardenia* for him. The name pertained to the Cape Jasmine Gardenia that is found in the vicinity of the Cape of Good Hope at the southern tip of Africa. *Fothergilla gardenia* also pertains to Alexander Garden.

In the *Aberdeen Magazine* of 1761, a description of the plant that Garden sent to Jane Colden appears. The article states,

Doctor Garden writes Doctor Whytt, that, in the summer 1754, he met, about a mile from the town of New York in New England, with a plant, which, at first, he took to be a *hypericum*, but, on examining it, found it different; upon which he took down its characters, and sent them, some days later, to Miss Jenny Colden (daughter of the Honourable Cadwallader Colden) a very ingenious young lady and curious Botanist. In return to this, Miss Colden sent Dr. Garden the characters of a plant which proves to be the same; it is No. 1533 of her collection, and was first found by her, Summer 1753. Using the privilege of a first discoverer, she was pleased to call the new plant *Gardenia*, in compliment to Dr. Garden.[87]

Alexander Garden's name remains engrained with those of John Mitchell and Cadwallader Colden in the taxonomy of the world's flora.

*   *   *

JANE COLDEN

Jane Colden, who, along with her father, exchanged letters, seeds, and descriptions with Garden, merits special recognition in a biography of Cadwallader Colden. Garden noted that Jane's descriptions of plants were often more detailed and accurate than those of her father.[88] Not only was she the first recognized female botanist in America and perhaps the entire world, but deserves the appellation "America's First Female Scientist." And all of her accomplishments took place within a brief period of time during the 1750s distant from any urban center and the halls of academia.

Jane, called Jenny by members of the family, the second oldest of the Coldens' daughters, was born in New York City on March 27, 1724, and moved to Coldengham with the family four years later.

Jane and her siblings were educated at home. Although Colden wrote to Franklin that "I think the power of a nation consists in the knowledge and virtue of its inhabitants,"[89] none of his children were sent to elementary school or to an institution of higher education. The correspondence of his children that is included in the volumes of *Collections of the New-York Historical Society* provides evidence that all of his children were literate and well-versed. It is generally assumed that Colden's wife played a major role in the education of the children because Cadwallader was often absent from the home. Of Mrs. Colden it is written, "She is said to have taught them habits of virtue and economy and gave them in her life and character the brightest of examples, so it can be presumed that her daughters were apt scholars in the accomplishments required of well-bred and trained gentlewomen of the day."[90] Jane, uniquely, stands out as her father's personally trained protégé as a botanist.

In 1755, Colden wrote to Gronovius,

I thought that Botany is an Amusement which may be made agreeable for the Ladies who are often at a loss to fill up their time if it could be made agreeable to them Their natural curiosity & the pleasure they take in the beauty & variety of dress seems to fit them for it The chief reason that few or none of them have hitherto applied themselves to this study I believe is because all the books of any value are wrote in Latin & and so filled with technical words that obtaining the necessary previous knowledge is so tiresome & disagreeable that they are discouraged at the first setting out & give it over before they can receive any pleasure in the pursuit

I have a daughter who has an inclination to reading & a curiosity for natural phylosophy or natural History & a sufficient capacity for attaining a competent knowledge I took the pains to explain Linnaeus's system & to put it in English for her use by freeing it from the Technical terms which was easily don by useing two or three words in place of one She is now grown very fond of the study and has made such progress in it as I believe would please you if you saw her performance Tho' perhaps she could not have been persuaded to learn the terms at first she now understands in some degree Linnaeus's characters notwithstanding that she does not understand Latin She has already a pretty large volume in writing of the Description of plants She has shewn a method of takeing the impression of the leaves on paper with printers ink by a simple kind of rolling press which is of use in distinguishing the species by their leaves No description in words alone can give so clear an Idea as when the description is assisted with a picture She has the impression of 300 plants in the manner you'l see by the sample sent you. That you may have some conception of her performance & manner of describing I propose to inclose some samples in her own writing some of which I think are new Genus's. . . .[91]

In addition to teaching Jane the process of making ink impressions of leaves on paper, Colden had books sent from England to augment her education. He wrote Collinson, "[I] . . . design likewise to send you a Sample of my daughter Jenny's performances in Botany. As it is not usual for woemen to take pleasure in Botany as a Science I shall do what I can to incourage her in this amusement which fills up her idle hours to much better purpose than the usual amusements eagerly pursued by others of her sex. As she [Jane] cannot have the opportunity of seeing plants in a Botanical Garden I think the next best is to see the best cuts or pictures of them for which purpose I would buy for her Tournefort's *Institutiones Herbariae*, Morison's *Historia Plantarum*, or if you know any better books for this purpose as you are a better judge than I am will be obliged to make this choice."[92] Collinson replied: "I have at last been So luckky to geyt you a fine Tournefort's *Herbal* & the *History of Plants* and Martin in excellent preservation to which have added 2 Volumes of *Edinburgh Essays* for the sake of the Curious Botanic Dissertation off your ingenious daughter being the Only Lady that I have yett heard of that is a professor of the Linnean System of which He is not a Little proud."[93]

Jane was also inspired by the visits to Coldengham of the notable colonial botanists, John and William Bartram and Alexander Garden, and also that of Peter Kalm of Sweden. Jane gained the respect of the community of botanists. In a letter from John Bartram to Collinson dated 1753 describing his visit, he wrote, "Got our dinner and set out to gather seeds, and did not get back till two hours within night; that looked over some of the Doctor's daughter's botanical, curious observations."[94] In 1756, Collinson wrote John Bartram that "Our friend Colden's daughter has, in a scientific manner sent over several sheets of plants, very curiously anatomized after his method. I believe she is the first lady that has attempted anything of this nature."[95] A year later, John Bartram responded to a letter from Jane indicating that "I am very careful of it, and it keeps company with the choicest correspondence."[96]

Jane's expertise qualified her to instruct the fourteen-year-old Samuel Bard in the science of botany. In 1756, Bard was sent by his father, a friend of Cadwallader Colden, to Coldengham as an escape from New York City because of the boy's ill health. In *A Domestic Narrative of the Life of Samuel Bard* it is written, "This residence not only restored him to good health, but filled his memory with pleasing recollections both of the society and studies to which it introduced him. In the family resided Miss Colden. . . . With this lady, differing in years but united in tastes, Mr. Bard formed an intimate friendship; under her instruction he became skillful in botanizing, a pursuit which remained to him a favorable amusement, and which owed, perhaps, a part of its attraction to the pleasing associations with which it was originally connected, since to the end of his life, he never mentioned the name of his instructress without some admiration or attachment."[97] Samuel Bard received his medical degree from Edinburgh and founded the first medical school in New York, King's College (now Columbia University College of Physicians and Surgeons) in 1765. Bard dedicated his thesis to Cadwallader Colden: "Samuel Bard wishes to dedicate these first fruits of his training to the Honorable Cadwallader Colden, Esquire, Lieutenant Governor of New York for the thousand benefits shown him publicly and privately. . . ."[98]

Jane evidenced confidence in her ability as a descriptive botanist and did not hesitate to differ with the authority of Linnaeus. With regard to *Polygala* (S'eneca or Snakeroot), she wrote, "Linnaeus describes this as being a Papilionatious Flower, and calls the two largest Leaves of the cup Alae, but as they continue, till the seed is ripe and the two flower Leaves, and its appendage folds [*sic*] together, I must beg leave to differ with him Added to this, the Seed Vessell, differs from all that I have observed of the Papilionatious Kind."[99] About *Clematis virginiana,* she indicated, "Neither Linnaeus take notice that there are some Plants of the Clematis that bear only Male flowers, but this I have observed with such care, that there can be no doubt of it."[100]

Jane's contributions to botany gained the respect of others with an established reputation. Collinson wrote Linnaeus, "What is marvelous his [Colden's] daughter is perhaps the first lady that has perfectly studied your system. She deserves to be celebrated." In a subsequent letter to Linnaeus, Collinson wrote, "Last week my friend, Mr. Ellis, wrote you a latter, recommending a curious botanic dissertation, by Miss Jane Colden. As this accomplished lady is the only one of the fair sex that I have heard of, who is scientifically skillful in the Linnaean system, you will no doubt distinguish her merits, and recommend her example to the ladies of every country." In the referred to letter, Ellis had stated, "The young lady merits your esteem and does honor to your system." He suggested that Linnaeus name a new genus for her, but that did not come to pass.[101]

All that remains of Jane Colden's botanical legacy is a manuscript that resided in the British Museum for over two hundred years, and is now in the manuscript section of the British Library. After her death it was acquired by Captain Frederick von

Wangenheim, a Prussian serving in a Hessian regiment during the American Revolution. It next passed on to Godfrey Baldinger, who was professor of botany and medical theory at the University of Göttingen and Marburg. It finally became the property of Joseph Banks, president of the Royal Society. On his death, it went with his collection of books and botanical specimens to the British Museum.[102]

A prefatory note by Wangenheim was published in an account of the manuscript in Schrader's *Journal für die Botanik* for 1800. The translation reads: "This MS., which has never been printed, contains a part of the New York Flora, and has been composed by a lady, the daughter of Governor Cadwallader Colden, well known for his botanical works, and also a physician. This lady married a doctor of medicine, Farquhar, a Scotchman by birth and she died soon afterwards. Some of the names are according to her father and according to Gronovius, and some are according to the Brandenburg doctor Schoepff, who has read this work. The trivial names are according to Linnaeus. This work is a remarkable one because it is that of a lady who possessed such a love for botany that she learned Latin, and judging by its nature is so worthy and correct that contains many even minute things." It was written in New York in May 1782.[103]

The title page identifies the author as the daughter of Cadwallader Colden; the name, Jane, is conspicuously absent.

FLORA
NOV.–EBORACENSIS.
Plantas in Solo Natali
collegit, descripsit,
delineavit,
COLDENIA,
Cadwallader Coldens
Filia.

The manuscript consists of 340 drawings, which are ink outlines washed in with neutral tint rather than the impressions referred to by Colden to Gronovius. The pages that include her written descriptions are numbered 1 to 341 but there are some pages with only the name of the plant on the top of the sheet. As noted by Britten, the descriptions are "excellent-full, careful and evidently taken from the living specimens." One of these (No. 153 of the manuscript) was published in *Essays and Observations*, vol. 2 (Edinburgh, 1770). It was the plant that had been sent to her by Garden, who found it in New York, and she had tried to have it named Gardenia by Linnaeus. Another of her descriptions, translated into Latin was published in the *Correspondence of Linnaeus*, vol. i., page 94.[104]

In her research, she conversed with the "Country People" and Indians, from whom she learned of the uses of some of the plants. A tea made of the leaves of the Mountain-mint (*Pycnanthemum incanum*) was used for stomach ailments. A preparation of the root of Goldthread (*Coptis trifolia*) was used for sore throat and canker sore. Prickly Ash (*Aralia spinosa*) was treatment for coughs and also dropsy (edema). Others were specified for use in cookery.[105] Jane is also credited with a 1756 memorandum of the process of making cheese on the farm.[106] Walter Rutherfurd, a Scottish officer who served in the French and Indian War and visited Coldengham in 1758, wrote, "She [Jane] makes the best cheese I ever ate in America."[107]

The period of Jane's dedication to botany ended abruptly with her marriage on March 12, 1759, to Dr. William Farquhar, a Scotsman, widower, and highly regarded practitioner of medicine in New York City. The couple met shortly after the Coldens moved to Flushing. Jane died on March 10, 1766 and her only child died the same year. The cause of her death and the death of her child were not reported.

Chapter 6

POLITICAL PEAK AND REPUTATIONAL NADIR

1759–1768

The year 1759 began with correspondence between Colden and William Smith, Jr., who would remain Colden's forceful antagonist throughout the decade, in spite of the friendship that had existed between Colden and Smith's father. A week after Colden read *The History of the Province of New-York, from the First Discovery to the Year MDCCXXXII (1732)* by William Smith, Jr., which was published in London in 1757, he took up his pen to vent his ire. Smith had included in the final chapter titled "From 1720 to the administration of Cosby" a consideration of Captain Campbell's attempt to procure land for himself and groups of immigrants whom he sponsored in the province in 1737 (see chapter 3, pp. 61 and 62). Although Colden's name was not mentioned, his involvement, in concert with Lt. Governor George Clarke, was obvious.

Colden stated in a letter to Smith, "It is in the principal part absolutely false & an egregious calumny of the persons, who at the time had the administration of Government in their hands. . . . The public defamation being an egregious injury to the public faith & honour of the Government of New York you know the proper method for redress that may be taken."[1]

Smith was adamant in affirming his interpretation of the

event, which he admitted took place when he was merely a boy. Two weeks after receiving Colden's letter, he wrote, "Your letter of the 15 January, which came to me unsealed, contains such a heavy Charge of Misrepresentation, Falsehood and Calumny, that I am almost inclined, to think myself relieved of the Obligation, which your Age, Rank, Character and particularly your professed Friendship to my Father, would otherwise undoubtedly, have laid me under, to take Notice of every Thing, wherein you might conceive yourself in the least Degree concerned."[2]

Smith's evidence was purely hearsay. It came to him from Campbell's wife by way of her son, who, in turn, gave it to James Alexander, who had been a member of the Council at the time of the event in 1737. In a letter written as a follow-up to Smith's correspondence, Colden correctly pointed out that the heads of the families who came over with Campbell refused to settle under his auspices, and that Campbell did not have the personal finances to purchase the 30,000 acres. As far as Alexander's personal interpretation was concerned, he completely absolved Colden and pointed out that Colden was not involved with the Council at the time of the event, almost twenty years previously.[3]

In a letter to his son Alexander, Colden expanded his remarks concerning Smith's *History of New York*. In that letter, Colden indicated that during his period of relative detachment from political affairs he was preparing his memoirs of the government of New York. He criticized Smith for attributing the removal of Colonel Schuyler and Mister Philipse from the Council to their opposition to the continuance of the Assembly. Rather, Colden stressed that the reason for their dismissal was that Schuyler had committed the king's seal to Philipse, who received it into his custody—a criminal act (see chapter 2, pp. 29 and 30).

In the letter, Colden continued with a chronicle of events that occurred during Governor Burnet's tenure. Colden recounted Burnet's refusal to qualify James Delancey after he had been elected a member of the Assembly. Delancey, based on his French and Dutch ancestry, was designated not to be a naturalized foreigner, which would have precluded his service. This generated intense party struggles that continued over the years. Colden described the Assembly at that time as consisting of individuals who deemed themselves to be unaccountable to any other authority and who were prone to spread slander and calumny. Colden concluded that "It is not fit that Mr. Smith's history should pass for a chronicle of New York" because "He is so assuming in his manner, especially in giving Characters, often unfair, allwise partial whether his characters be favorable or otherwise, continually biased by his connections, either as to family, political party or religious sect, that some resentment is unavoidable."[4]

While Colden remained in Flushing at the house he had rented in 1757, relatively disengaged from political activities throughout 1759 and the first nine months of 1760, the British forces continued on their victorious course over the French. On June 26, 1759, Fort Ticonderoga was taken by Major General Jeffrey Amherst, who replaced General James Abercromby as the commander-in-chief of all British forces in North America. The French commandant of the fort ordered the fortifications destroyed and the troops to withdraw to the Isle-au-Nuits in Lake Champlain. On August 1, Amherst learned that Crown Point had been abandoned. Troops were stationed there and the French withdrew completely from Lake Champlain. The formidable Fort Niagara also fell without a battle on July 25. The British took possession of forts at Venango, Le Boeuf, and Presque Isle, leaving Fort Pontchartrain at Detroit as the only fort in the Lake Erie area under French control.

The most definitive battle of the French and Indian War took place on the morning of September 13, 1759, and lasted about fifteen minutes. The British engaged and soundly defeated the French on the Plains of Abraham at Quebec. The articles of capitulation were signed on September 18. A year later Montreal surrendered without a battle, and, a week after that event, the British flag was raised at the Detroit fort, thereby gaining for Great Britain sole control of North America.

In 1760, Colden penned an essay directed at his nephew who was to embark on a new educational endeavor. The essay entitled "An Introduction to the Study of Phylosophy" summarized Colden's views on both philosophy and science. He emphasized the need to expand one's knowledge in the context of society. Colden paints a self-portrait of his intellectual profile in his conclusion. "The gentleman, who proposes to be generally useful in society, ought not to fix his thought single on one branch of science, but to have a competent knowledge of the principles of every branch. . . . While he reads and thinks by turns, he should in the intervals, cultivate his intellectual faculties by general conversation, where he may obtain more useful knowledge than can be learned from books."[5]

On June 10, 1760, the Assembly, under the leadership of Lieutenant Governor Delancey passed several bills, the most significant of which was the regulation of the practice of "Physic and Medicine."[6] Colden is generally credited with being the force behind the passage of that bill, in which it was specified that an exam was required by those aspiring to practice. This was the first act in the colonies to regulate the practice of medicine, but it was limited to the City of New York and contained a grandfather clause, excusing all those currently practicing medicine.[7]

On July 29, Delancey engaged in interviews with several politicians on Staten Island and returned that evening. The following morning he was found gasping in a chair at home and died, presumably as a result of asthma of which he suffered for years. Smith's assessment of Delancey's contributions to the colony was most complimentary. Smith wrote, "Upon the whole, his accomplishments rendered him an ornament to the country which gave him birth. None of his predecessors possessed natural talents superior, if equal to his. . . ."[8]

Colden's life underwent an immediate and dramatic change. In his seventy-third year, he came out of retirement and took up residence in Government House at Fort George (currently, the location of the National Museum of the American Indian in Lower Manhattan), as president of the Council. Colden assumed the title of President of the Council and Commander-in-Chief of the Province of New York.

He received congratulatory letters from several of the colonial governors, including James Hamilton of Pennsylvania, Francis Fauquier of Virginia, Horatio Sharpe of Maryland, and William Bull of South Carolina. He also received congratulatory correspondence from Alexander Garden and Benjamin Franklin, who was in London at the time. In a letter, written from his encampment site on the shore of the St. Lawrence River near Isle Royale, Major General Amherst offered condolences for the death of Delancey, and wrote, "Sir, it some what Alleviates my Grief to find that the Reins of Government have devolved on a Person of so much Experience as Yourself, not doubting but I shall find the same Zeal in You that I have always met with in your Predecessor. . . ."[9]

Colden used his position to advance his sons. This is evidenced in a letter from the Earl of Halifax to Peter Collinson dated October 12, 1760. The earl wrote, "I was pleased that upon the Death of Lieutenant Governor Delancey, the Administration, of Governm^t devolved upon Mr Colden, whose experience, public service and Integrity I have been long Acquainted with. My only doubt was whither his Age might not make it burthensome to him. . . . I should be very glad to oblige both him and you by making his Son one of the Council, but, when I state then to you, I am Satisfied you will be Sensible of the Weight of the Objections there are to it at present. . . ."[10]

On October 22, Colden addressed the Assembly in his new position for the first time. He assured the members that he would concur with them in "every measure conducive to the prosperity of the colony."[11] One week later, the General Assembly issued a formal response, in which the members asserted that they "shall cheerfully contribute our utmost assistance to every measure conducive to the ease of your administration, & the true Interest of the People we represent."[12] The session lasted until November 8, when Colden signed the nineteen proposed bills without a single objection, including one that provided him a salary of 1,800 pounds per year.[13]

King George II died on October 25 and his grandson, George III, rose to the throne. In November the City of New York received Major General Amherst as a triumphal hero, and, with much pomp and circumstance, presented him with the "freedom of their municipality."[14] Throughout the winter, self-congratulations over the recent victory, accompanied by pervasive optimism and patriotism, dominated. This temporarily obscured the previous political polarization. But the arrival of the spring would be accompanied by the early harbingers of a storm that would eventuate in the elevation of Colden to an unenviable position as the most vilified individual in the history of colonial New York, if not in all of the colonies.

The year of 1760 represented a watershed in Colden's life. The most contemporary report of the administrations of Lieutenant Governor Colden and Governor Monckton covered the period between 1760 and 1762, and was written by William Smith, Jr., for the second volume of his *The History of the Province of New-York*. The chronicle is obviously biased because Smith had been and continued to be one of Colden's severest critics. Smith was a member of the legal profession, for which Colden had little regard and a distinct antipathy. At the time, the three legal leaders in the New York colony were Smith, John Morin Scott, and William Livingston. Smith and Livingston had been educated together at Yale, and they were joined by Scott in Smith's father's law office. They were populists who were opposed to absolute rule by the monarchy. They organized the Whig Club in 1752, and held weekly meetings at the King's Arms Tavern, where the walls reverberated with words of independence and the leveling of society, an absolute anathema for Colden.[15]

After George II died and the new king was crowned, the New York lawyers invoked an unwritten law that mandated the dissolution of extant assemblies and the election of new members. An election took place and little change in the membership resulted. In May, there was a two-week session of the new Assembly, during which the members voted that the laws enacted between the death of the late king and the receipt of notification by the Assembly required legalization. Colden objected because it was contrary to royal and parliamentary instructions, and that it was absurd to restrain a lawful act based on lack of knowledge, which was impossible to attain at the time. He added that the bill would have given lawyers an overriding power.[16]

The second and more contentious bill indicated that the selection of judges should be independent of the Crown and that the judges of the Supreme Court were to be appointed on the basis of their good behavior. Colden continued his loyalty to the Crown, and offered the chief justice's position to Smith, Sr., who refused. Colden then declared that the renewal of the other positions was dependent upon the Crown. Smith, Jr., in his history, deemed Colden's action to be "universally disgustful."[17] Other unpopular actions of Colden included the curtailment of the illicit trade that had taken place for many years between New York merchants and the French West Indies, and the overturning of land patents that he contended had been granted in violation of instructions from the Crown.[18]

Although local antagonism toward Colden intensified, he was rewarded by the king with the long-desired position of lieutenant governor. The commission that was dated April 14, 1761, stated,

> GEORGE the Third, by the Grace of God, of Great Britain France and Ireland, King Defender of the Faith &c[2] To Our Trusty and Well beloved Cadwallader Colden Esquire GREETING, WE, reposing especial Trust and Confidence inn your Loyalty,

Integrity and Ability, do by these Presents constitute and appoint you to be Our Lieutenant Governor of Our Province of New York and the Territories depending thereon in America, in the room of James Delancey Esquire deceased.[19]

On May 12, 1761, Colden leased a 120 acre farm, located about a mile and a half south of the village of Flushing, Long Island, from John and Thomas Willet. A year later, Colden purchased the land and over the ensuing two years built a mansion, which he named Spring Hill (fig. 9).[20]

Figure 9. "Spring Hill" in Flushing, Long Island. Photo taken 1924. Courtesy of New York Historical Society.

On October 19, 1761, the British warship *Alcide* arrived in New York with the commission for the new governor, Major General Robert Monckton. The thirty-five-year-old Monckton had a distinguished military career in the War of the Austrian Succession and, more recently, in the Seven Years (French and Indian) War. In 1755, he led the siege that captured Fort Beauséjour, and was named lieutenant governor of Nova Scotia after that victory. He held that position for three years. In 1759, he was appointed second in command to General James Wolfe for the battle of Quebec. On the Plains of Abraham, Monckton commanded the British right flank and sustained a chest wound. He was reassigned to New York for convalescence. In 1760, he was appointed commander of the British forces in the provinces south of New York.

At the time of his appointment as governor of New York, Monckton was in command of troops stationed at Staten Island in anticipation of an expedition to the West Indies. The process of the swearing in of the new governor provided a new occasion for Colden's reputation to be compromised by his political foes. The process called for the governor-elect to formally produce his commission and instructions in Council, after which he was sworn in. On the day, which Monckton had selected for his inauguration, Colden became acquainted with the fact that the instructions had not arrived, and he called for a delay. Colden's persistent nemesis, William Smith, Jr., told Monckton that Colden had known of the absence of the instructions previously and was using the situation to delay the taking of the oath.[21] The inauguration proceeded on the originally designated day.

Nineteen days later Monckton sailed with an expeditionary force under his command directed for the capture of Martinique, which surrendered on February 3, 1762. Colden governed New York during Monckton's absence. Monckton returned to New York in June, and assumed his leadership role. He held the position of governor until June 1765 despite leaving New York permanently in June 1763.

Before Monckton left for Martinique, he wrote Colden that in his absence Colden should receive "one full moiety [i.e., half] of the Salary, and of all Perquisites," which the governor would have received, during his absence.[22] Colden informed Monckton that he disagreed and that Governor Burnett, during his tenure, had indicated to him that "the Lieutenant Governor, President of the Council &c, exercising the Administration of Government, upon the Absence or the Death of the Governor in Chief, should have *one half of the Salary, and all Perquisites & Emoluments of Government.*"[23] Monckton maintained his original assertion that "half" rather than "all" perquisites was appropriate.[24]

Colden solicited the assistance of John Watts, a member of the Council. They conjointly drew up an agreement by which half the profits of government were to be paid to Colden and half to the deputy-secretary in trust for Monckton. Monckton countered with the proposal that, while Colden was in charge, everything was to be paid to the deputy-secretary until Monckton's return. At that time, if specific instructions indicated that the profits were to be divided, Monckton would comply; if not, he would keep all. Colden ignored this, considering it an insult to his character. Smith then drew up an agreement that, if Colden's contention proved to be correct, he would be paid, but was required to submit an accounting under oath, which even Monckton thought was not necessary. Smith's action added to Colden's consideration of his antagonist as "a crafty, malicious smooth-tongued hypocrite."[25]

Five days after Monckton's departure for the West Indies, Colden opened a new session of the Assembly with a passionate plea for expediting justice and reducing the expense, thereby allowing him the opportunity to focus on one of his criticisms, that of the bench and the bar. The Assembly sarcastically responded with the statement, "As the complaints your honor mentions probably arise from the want of a *legal* establishment of fees, we cannot help thinking a general establishment of the fees of *all the officers of the government* will put a stop to these, as well to several other complaints of the like nature."[26]

One bill, which granted salaries to the judges on condition of their acceptance during good behavior, Colden amended to provide fixed salaries for the judges appointed under the new tenure. It was eventually approved. The bill, legalizing the acts of the legislature between the death of George II and its announcement in America was not brought up for reconsideration. A bill authorizing the partition of land grants and the establishment of provision, similar to one that Colden had successfully proposed forty years previously, was introduced. Colden signed a compromised bill after his amendments were added.

Smith ended the final chapter in his *History*, on "The Administrations of Colden and Monckton" with a parting barb:

> Mr. Hardy . . . who by renewing the judge's commissions during good behavior, taught this colony to believe that it was choice and some sinister motive, and not a dread of administration that prompted Mr. Colden to stickle for a dispensation of justice under the control of the Crown. It was therefore with a malignant pleasure that the public soon after the session discovered Mr. Colden's late promotion to the rank of Lieutenant Governor was not the reward of merit, but the effort of low craft and condescension and fraud. To gain an interest with Mr. John Pownall, a clerk to the Board of Trade, who had the ear of the earl of Halifax, and to raise the idea of his being able to influence the Assembly, he offered him the agency of the colony—a bait to which the minister could not be indifferent."[27]

The year 1762 was one of great personal loss for Colden. In March his wife of forty-seven years died at Government House, and in June his thirty-one- yearold unmarried daughter, Catherine, also died.[28] The year was relatively non-confrontational for Colden.

The correspondence of the next year was initiated by a letter from Benjamin Franklin, who reported on the discovery that Quicksilver was a melted metal, that cooling could be effected by evaporation, that he was experimenting with magnetism, and that, while in England, he had invented a new musical instrument [the glass armonica].[29] In September a letter from the Earl of Halifax expressed concern over an argument between two New York merchants named Mr. Forsey and Mr. Cunningham that resulted in Cunningham stabbing Forsey. Colden was instructed to report if a trial resulted in a conviction. If conviction ensued, Colden was instructed to delay judgment and execution until the Crown considered the matter.[30]

Cunningham had previously lost a civil action suit for assault and battery against Forsey. Cunningham was then turned down by the Supreme Court for a review. John Tabor Kempe, who served at the last attorney general for the province of New York (1759–1782), wrote Colden that "On the whole Sir as I humbly conceive the Kings Intent to be, that only Errors in the Law and not matters of Fact tried on Appeal, I think a Writ of Error only should issue to bring the proceedings before your Honor and the Council. . . ."[31] Daniel Horsmanden, the chief justice of the province, stated, "An Attempt then to re-examine the Verdict of a Jury, is repugnant to the Laws both of England and this Colony."[32]

Colden, however, stayed the court's judgment and asked the chief justice to send him the proceedings, arguing that the case was poorly managed. The case was resolved in 1765 when the New York Assembly supported the Supreme Court decision, and the Board of Trade agreed. The constitutional controversy intensified the alienation of Colden by the moderate party and the conservative merchant coalition. The entire populace detested Colden for his unwavering support of the Crown and it was stated that "the old Body was always dislik'd enough, but now they would prefer Beelzebub himself to him."[33]

Most of the correspondence during 1764, as incorporated in *Colden's Papers*, is related to Indian affairs and emanated from the pen of Sir William Johnson, who served as the British superintendent of Indian affairs for the northern colonies, and, after emerging as the hero of the Battle of Lake George in 1755, was the first colonial to be made a baronet. The Treaty of Paris was signed at Versailles on February 10, 1763. Although it declared that France surrendered all her possessions east of the Mississippi River, the Indians remained hostile. In April 1763, several tribes banded together under the leadership of Pontiac. In an effort to regain control of the Ohio Valley, they harassed the frontiersman and their families and took possession of several forts and outposts. Forts Pitt and Detroit were blockaded.

In August troops commanded by Colonel Henry Bouquet defeated the Indians at the Battle of Bushy Run, thus ending the blockade of Fort Pitt. The Indians lost their enthusiasm for battle and Pontiac capitulated on October 31, 1763. On April 3, 1764, at Johnson Hall in the Mohawk Valley, Johnson signed a peace treaty with the Seneca nation. In August Johnson wrote Colden that he had met with about two thousand Indians including all the chiefs of the Western Nations with the exception of Pontiac and the Six Nations. Many of their disputes with each other and with the provincials were settled.[34] The Assembly deliberated on the validity of the patents for land in the colony and the fairness of previous purchases from the Indians, but determined that they could make no change.[35]

During that year, Colden's correspondence attested to the efficacy of Franklin's lightning rod. The steeple of Trinity Church in New York was struck with lightning and no damage resulted. By contrast, lightning also struck one of the corners fifty to sixty feet below the top of the spire, and this caused an urn below that corner, which was not furnished with a conducting rod, to shatter.[36]

On April 5, 1764, during the time that the colonies were in the midst of an economic depression, Parliament passed the Sugar Act, which taxed sugar and also lumber that could be sent only to Great Britain. The New York Assembly wrote Colden: "We hope your Honour will join us, in an Effort to secure that great Badge of English Liberty, of being taxed only with our Consent; to which, we conceive, all His Majesty's Subjects at home and abroad equally entitled, and also in pointing out to the Ministry, the many mischiefs arising from the Act, commonly called the Sugar Act, to both us and Great Britain."[37] Colden refused to sign. The act was repealed in 1766.

In August Colden received this first notification of the act, which would lead to his vilification. The Earl of Halifax, secretary of state for the Northern Department, sent a communiqué dated August 11, 1764, stating,

> The House of Commons having, in the last session of Parliament, come to a resolution by which it is declared that towards defraying the necessary Expenses of defending, protecting & securing the British Colonies & Plantations in America, it may be proper to charge certain Stamp Duties in the said Colonies & Plantations, It is His Majesty's Pleasure, that you should transmit to me without delay, a List of all Instruments made use of in publick Transactions, Law Proceedings, Grants, Conveyances, Securities of Land or money, within your Government with proper & sufficient descriptions of the same, in order that if Parliament should think proper to pursue the Intention of the aforesaid Resolution, they may thereby by enabled to carry it into Execution, in the most effectual & least bothersome Manner."[38]

In October, on learning of the proposed Stamp Act, the New York Assembly sent a petition to Parliament that was so forceful and argumentative that no member of Parliament would introduce it.[39]

The year 1765 is identifiable as the period that sealed Colden's reputation as the ultimate Loyalist and the major enemy of the populace. The events of that year moved his intellectual contributions backstage to a point of insignificance. His participation in the year's political processes would eventually erase any positive appreciation on the impact he made during an unrivaled longevity of service to the province of New York. He would emerge from the fray as a reviled historical irritant that provided yet another stimulus for independence and democracy.

Colden's correspondence that year began, emblematically, with an extensive written opinion on legal appeals. In answering the question, "Whether the King by the 32^d Article of Instructions to his Captain General hath given an appeal to all Civil Courses from the Courts of Common Law to his Governor and Council and whether his Majesty by his said Instruction constituted his Governor and Council a Court for hearing and determining of such appeals," Colden drew from English history, beginning with the Magna Carta, to support his stance in the Forsey/Cunningham case.[40] Colden's legal action sensitized the public and indirectly fanned the flames that would erupt nine months later.

In his role as lieutenant governor he continued his efforts at achieving peace with the Indians and fairness for them in their land negotiations with settlers. He was in constant contact by means of mail with the agent for Indian affairs, William Johnson, with whom Colden shared a common goal. Peace was formalized with the Delaware and Susquehanna tribes. Colden also continued cooperating with Major General Amherst by providing support for the troops stationed in New York as protection for the population.

The history of events leading up to Colden's ultimate crisis can be dated to 1763. That year, George Grenville became the prime minister of Great Britain, which was confronted with significant financial problems consequent to the cost of the French and Indian War and the need to maintain a large peaceful establishment in its American colonies. The Crown and Parliament expected the colonists to contribute to the cost of their own defense. The first tax to raise the required money was the Sugar Act of 1764. The colonists objected for economic reasons, but, initially did not invoke the issue of taxation without representation.

The Sugar Act was replaced by the Stamp Act, which was passed by Parliament on March 22, 1765, with an implementation date of November 1. The highest tax was placed on attorney's licenses. Papers related to court proceedings and land grants were also taxed, as were newspapers, pamphlets, and cards. The stamps had to be purchased with scarce hard currency rather than more available colonial paper currency. Admiralty courts, which were controlled by England, were given jurisdiction over violators. The tax brought into focus the issue of taxation without representation. Before the year ended, all of the colonies except North Carolina and Georgia sent protests from their Assemblies to Parliament, often emphasizing the issue of taxation without representation.[41]

When the act was passed stamp distributors were appointed for each of the colonies. On August 14, 1765, Andrew Oliver, Massachusetts's distributor, was hanged in effigy and his house was looted. He resigned the next day.[42] Within days, James Evers, New York's distributor of stamps, resigned for fear of "the greatest risk of my Person and Fortune . . . to Prevent the same Cruel Fate Mr Oliver met with at Boston."[43]

The Council of New York met on September 4, 7, and 9 relative to the Stamp Act.[44] At the first meeting, Evers's letter of resignation was presented by Colden. At the second meeting, in response to a query from General Gage, commander-in-chief of his majesty's forces in North America, regarding the need for military support, the Council indicated that there was no need for alarm that riots would develop in the colony. At the third meeting, the city's mayor affirmed the Council's opinion that no precaution was necessary. In September the governor of Connecticut indicated to Colden that he had no desire to receive that stamps that were allocated to his colony,[45] and the governor of New Jersey followed suit.[46] On October 23, the Council was informed that the ship bearing the stamped paper had arrived at New York Harbor and the next day it anchored in the North River. On October 31, Colden took an oath, which was administered by the Council, to uphold "An Act for granting and applying certain Stamp Duties in the British Colonies and Plantations in America, towards defraying the Expenses of defending protecting and Securing the same. . . ."[47]

On Friday evening, November 1, an anonymous notice was delivered to Colden at Fort George. It stated,

"Sir,

The People of this City & Province of New York, have been inform'd y^t you bound yourself under an Oath to be the Chief Murderer of their Rights & Privileges, by acting as an Enemy to your King and Country to Liberty & Mankind in the Inforcement of the Stamp-Act which we are unanimously determined shall never take Place among us, so long as Man has Life to defend his injured Country – Thus wicked men of old conspired ag^t Paul an Apostle of J. Christ, and bound themselves under a Curse, that they would neither eat nor drink, till they killed him; but God defeated their Bloody Purposes, as we trust he'll do yours, and Paul was deliver'd. How it fared with his intended assassins History does not certainly inform us; but we can with certainty assure you of your Fate if you do not this Night Solemnly make Oath before a Magistrate & publish to the People, that you never will, directly nor indirectly, by any Act of yours or any Person under your Influence, endeavor to introduce of or execute the Stamp-Act, or any Part of it, that you will to the utmost of your power prevent it taking Effect here, and endeavor to obtain a Repeal of it in England. So help you God.

We have heard of your Design of Menace to fire upon the Tow, in Case of Disturbance, but assure yourself, that, if you dare to Perpetrate and such murderous Act, you'll bring tour grey Hairs with Sorrow to the Grave, You'll die a Martyr to your own Villany, & be Hang'd, like Porteis [Porteous] upon a Sign-Post, as a Memento to all wicked Governors, and that every Man, that assists you, Shall be, surely, put to Death. [48]

At a meeting of the Council on November 2, Colden reported that, on the previous night, his two sleighs, his sedan chair, his own and several other carriages in the stables adjacent the fort were taken and burned by the mob.[49] Colden was hanged in effigy and the elegant home of Major Thomas James, the commander of the garrison at Fort George, was sacked. The Council, which had previously received word that Sir Henry Moore was appointed governor of the province, was unanimously in favor of temporizing any related action until the new governor could act. On November

5, the stamps were deposited in the City Hall to be guarded by the City Watch.[50] Anarchy was stemmed and relative calm returned.

Governor Moore arrived at New York on November 13. Colden immediately turned over the command as well as the residence and moved to the house of his grandson, Stephen Delancey, where he remained for five days. He then took a ferry to Spring Hill in Flushing. Moore, immediately, sought to establish his popularity and distanced himself from Colden. In February 1766, Colden wrote Henry Seymour Conway, secretary of the Northern Department, that Moore had totally neglected him "as could not but shagreen a person who had immediately preceded him in the chief command, and having ordered the Fort to be dismantled without consulting me, I thought it proper for me to retire to the Country. . . . My tiring seemed very agreeable to him & I took my leave."[51]

In December 1765, the lawyers of New York proceeded to execute their business without the use of stamps. On December 13, Colden sent a summation, entitled "State of the Province of New York," to the secretary of state and Board of Trade. In the document, he indicated that there were four classes— great land owners, lawyers, merchants, and farmers. He described their relationships with one and other, and with the provincial government and Great Britain. Colden also offered his conclusions regarding the controversies of his administration and his judgment of the Stamp Act.[52] That year, Colden published his *Treatise on Wounds and Fevers*, considered to be his most notable medical contribution and the authoritative work at the time.[53]

In February 1766, Colden was surprised to receive a letter from Henry Seymour Conway, secretary of state, who had been an opponent of the Stamp Act, in which he expressed the king's and Parliament's disapproval of Colden's decision to act on the previous November 2 and await the arrival of Governor Moore.[54] On February 21, Parliament repealed the Stamp Act and the king gave his assent on March 17. It was replaced by the face saving Declaratory Act, which affirmed Parliament's right to tax the colonies. An extension of the 1765 Quartering Act, which required the provision of lodgings and supplies for British troops in America, was also passed in 1766. The New York Assembly refused to comply. In November, one year after the riot, Colden was still awaiting words of commendation and payment for his losses. He composed a detailed report of vindication that he sent to Collinson, requesting that 120 copies be printed, twenty to be sent to Colden and the remainder to be sent to members of Parliament.[55]

During the next two years, Moore continued to actively oversee the political activities of New York while Colden remained in Flushing, devoid of significant influence or impact. In compliance with the Parliament's Septennial Act that mandated elections every seven years, a new Assembly was constituted. The Whig interests of the legal profession and city merchants were reduced. Judge Livingston's influence was also minimized. Colden's grandson was elected as the representative from Westchester.

In December Judge Livingston read to members of the Assembly from an anonymous printed pamphlet entitled "The Conduct of Cadwallader Colden, Esquire, Late Lieutenant Governor of New York, relating to the Judges Commissions, Appeals to the King and the Stamp Act." Livingston strongly censured the contained criticism, and a joint committee of the Council and Assembly was appointed to investigate. The committee reaffirmed Livingston's censure and stated that the document contained, "the most malignant aspersion upon the inhabitants of this colony in general," and it contributed "to destroy[ing] the Confidence of the people in two branches of the legislature and in the officers concerned in the due administration of justice; to render the government odious and contemptible; to abate due respect to authority, which was so necessary to peace and good order; to excite disadvantageous suspicions and jealousies in the minds of the people of Great Britain against his Majesty's subjects in this colony; and to expose the colony in general to resentments of the Crown and both houses of parliament."[56]

New York's economy was depressed, and there was an insufficient supply of circulating money. Embezzlement by the treasurer was discovered and counterfeiting was widespread. The New York Chamber of Commerce was established in 1768, and it immediately attempted to regulate the circulated currencies.[57]

In July the recently appointed secretary of state, the Earl of Hillsborough, directed Governor Moore to compensate Colden for losses sustained during the disturbances in New York. Hillsborough referred to Colden as "a Meritorious old Servant of the Crown."[58] The same month the past prime minister, George Grenville wrote Colden,

> The attack which you complain of as made upon yourself, seems to me to be a Severe one, & if owing to the Causes you asking for it, deserves to be enquired into, but as on the one hand you have the strongest Title to be supported for doing your Duty, so on the other those you complain of have a Right to be heard before They are censur'd. Your Behavior during the former Disturbances appeared to me to be highly meritorious & I have more than once declared to the House of Commons my Opinion concerning it. This Sir, is a Justice due to you, which as far as it depends upon me, I should always be ready to pay, & I am therefore very Sorry that you have felt so much uneasiness at a Time of Life which should naturally call, as you truly observe, for Quiet & Retirement, after so many years spent in public service."[59]

Moore complied with Hillsborough's order and presented Colden's account to the new Assembly. They voted to only provide Colden with his unpaid salary, but they refused to compensate him for his personal losses.

Chapter 7

AN OCTOGENARIAN

1769–1776

*C*olden remained an active political participant during the eight years of his ninth decade of life, at a time when the mean life expectancy of a North American colonist was thirty-five years. In the final segment of his life, he served under three governors of the province of New York, and ran the colony during interregnums and the governors' absences. The eight years included a final personal confrontation, in which he, once again, defended his principles and purse. During the same period, colonists witnessed battles with bloodshed, urban occupation by the British, and pan-colonial assertions that evolved into the American Revolution and the colonies' declaration of independence from British control. Colden's ultimate period of retirement was brief. After he died, his presence, contributions, and influence rapidly faded into obscurity, where they remained, with the exception of sporadic consideration.

In July 1769, Lord Hillsborough, secretary of state for the colonies, wrote to Sir Henry Moore, the governor of New York, indicating the Crown's displeasure with the Assembly's resolution against the importation of goods from Great Britain. Concern was also expressed for Assembly's extension of the jurisdiction of county courts and the concomitant limitation of the Supreme Court.[1]

After serving for four relatively peaceful years during which he enjoyed the respect of the populace and politicians, Moore suddenly died on September 11, leaving Colden in charge of the province. In early December, Colden received word that James Murray, the Earl of Dunmore, had been appointed governor of New York.[2] Dunmore's commission was formalized on January 2, 1770. Once again, Colden became the object of the king's disapproval. Hillsborough chastised Colden for a speech to the Assembly in which he stated that it was probable that the duties previously imposed by Parliament would be removed. The Crown also deemed inappropriate the steps taken by Moore and Colden in respect to the passage of a Paper Currency Bill. Hillsborough included in his correspondence, "The merit however of your former Services and what you say in respect to the time fixed by the Act for its operation which you state as an excuse for your Conduct, prevail with His Majesty to forbear any further Marks of His Displeasure, trusting that you will not for the future suffer yourself to be withdrawn from your Duty by and motive whatever."[3] A reminder of the premise of immutable loyalty to the Crown was presented in August 1770 with the unveiling of a large equestrian statue of George III at Bowling Green, in lower New York.

In 1770, just before Dunmore arrived in New York, the councilors and city members of the Assembly almost unanimously voted against a proposal to disallow the importation of goods from Great Britain.[4] Ten months after his appointment, the Earl of Dunmore arrived in New York on October 18. He served as New York's governor for less than a year, when he moved on to become the governor of Virginia in 1771. When Dunmore arrived, Colden retired to Spring Hill. Colden left with, what was for him, a relatively unique sense of appreciation by the city's merchants and ministers and members of the established church.

The issue of Colden's salary and perquisites during the period that he served as lieutenant governor while awaiting Dunmore's arrival was the genesis of Colden's final contentious encounter. For Colden, this represented the recurrence of a situation that was addressed and argued during General Monckton's gubernatorial tenure.

In November 1770, John Tabor Kempe, the attorney general of New York, filed a bill in Chancery, on behalf of the Crown, against Colden.[5] The specific point of contention was whether Colden, as lieutenant governor was entitled to a "Moiety" (half) of the "Perquisites and Emoluments" of the office of the leader of the province during the period of absence of the governor. Lengthy, detailed notes by Colden provide evidence of his step-by-step rebuttals of his opponents', namely, the Crown's and Lord Dunmore's, arguments.[6]

In reference to his opponents' invocation of a related declaration, which was made by King William in 1698, Colden insisted that the declaration died with the king, and was, therefore, null and void. Colden also contended that it was absurd to draw any conclusion from that royal declaration because the current salary of the governor and lieutenant governor were appropriated and bestowed by the provincial Assembly rather than the Crown or Parliament. Colden asserted that nothing specified that he, as lieutenant governor, was to receive a proportion of his salary, perquisites, and emoluments for the use of the king. Nor was a lieutenant governor accountable for his salary, bonds, bills and lands, which he had taken. Colden pointed out that there was no evidence that the king had given Lord Dunmore authority to execute any claim. Similarly, there was no authority, which had been granted to the attorney general to institute a suit in Chancery. Colden also contended that nothing related to the king's revenue or debts could be determined in Chancery, where Lord Dunmore was the sole judge.

Colden stressed that any and all the monies and profits, which he might have received, could be discovered in a court of common law. Once again, as was the case during a previous and similar disagreement at the time of Monckton's tenure, Colden insisted that the lieutenant governor, when acting in lieu of an absent governor, was entitled to *one half of the Salary and of all Perquisites and Emoluments of Government*. It had been assumed that the insertion of the word "of" before "all Perquisites and Emoluments" was a clerical error.

Colden agreed that "one half of the salary" was appropriate because it flowed from a royal bounty and the king could direct it to be paid in any proportion that he saw fit. By contrast, he argued that "Perquisites and Emoluments" were paid by individuals for services performed and, consequently, not under the king's purview. Colden proceeded to support his argument by parsing the specifics of the Declaration of King William, which had been invoked by his opponents. Colden pointed out that the declaration *"reserves to the King the disposal of the other Moiety of the said Salary."* No mention is made of "a Moiety of Perquisites and Emoluments." This was offered as enforcement of Colden's contention that the interpolated "of" was not meant to be.

The paper trail concerning the issue of Colden's perquisites continued in 1771 with a petition written by Colden's nemesis, William Smith, Jr., in his role as counsel for Lord Dunmore, who had assumed the position of governor of Virginia. The letter was addressed to Dunmore's replacement, Governor William Tryon.[7] Dunmore's counsel indicated that the king had the right to regulate and disperse the receipts of perquisites and emoluments, and that his client should receive half the perquisites and emoluments that Colden had collected during the period between Dunmore's commission and his arrival to assume the post in New York. In order to strengthen his case, Dunmore asked the justices of the Supreme Court for an opinion. They declared that Colden's argument was well-founded, and the case was dropped.[8]

William Tryon, who had been serving as the governor of North Carolina, was commissioned to change venues and replace Dunmore as the governor of New York, where he arrived on July 8, 1771. Prior to his arrival, Colden, in the role of lieutenant governor, presented a petition to establish a hospital in the city by favoring the incorporation of "The Society of the Hospital in the City of New-York in America" to the Council. The event brought together the actions of Samuel Bard and Colden, who had established a relationship fifteen years previously when a boyhood Bard recuperated from an illness at Coldengham in 1754. King's College had been established as a medical school in 1767 with Bard as the professor of the theory and practice of medicine. At the graduation of the first class in 1769, Bard inaugurated a campaign for the building of a hospital.[9] In 1771, King George III granted the charter and Colden, as lieutenant governor, signed the charter for what would become the second oldest hospital in the United States.

Between the time of Tryon's arrival and his departure for a temporary visit to England, Colden remained in Spring Hill, where he was detached from political activities. In 1772, he was elected as an honorary member of the Marine Society of New York, a charitable and educational organization that had been chartered by King George III in 1770 to "improve maritime knowledge and relieve indigent and distressed shipmasters, their widows and orphans. . . ." Colden's certificate reads,

> The Marine Society of this City which owes to you its Existence Impressed with the Warmest Gratitude for their Founder,—and Remembering also the Protection and Countenance, you have always shewn them, both in your publick and private Character, Think it their duty to give some lasting Testimony of these their Sentiments—this the Society could not be better effected than by the Unanimous Choice of you as a member of that Charitable Institution, which was formed under your Wise and benevolent Administration; a Choice, which at the same time that affords some Proof of their great respect for Lieutenant Governor Colden, reflects also particular Honour on themselves, by the addition of a Person of your Rank and Experience to their Society.[10]

Sometime in 1771 and 1772, Matthew Pratt painted two full-length portraits of Cadwallader Colden as an octogenarian, one standing alone (fig. 10) and the other with his grandson, Warren Delancey (fig. 11). In 1773, a third generation of the Colden family assumed the position of surveyor general of New York when Lord North, in response to a request from Colden coupled with an endorsement by Tryon, directed the appointment of Richard Nicholls Colden to succeed his father, Alexander.[11]

In his first demonstration of leadership, Governor Tryon succeeded in having the Assembly appropriate funds for quartering British troops in the province, and also established a militia. A period of relative calm in New York was altered by Parliament's passage of the Tea Act, which was signed by the king on May 10, 1773. It was designed to improve the financial status of the East India Company. Tea was to be shipped directly to the colonies and sold at a bargain price. Although a new tax was not imposed, the Townshend Duties were still in place, and the colonists regarded the Tea Act as an emphasis of the right of Parliament to tax without representation. The act granted the East India Company the right to directly ship its tea to the colonies as a duty-free export. The direct sale would effectively undercut the business of the local merchants.

Tryon planned to have the tea stored at Fort George but the Sons of Liberty, led by Alexander McDougall, vehemently objected to landing any tea. When Tryon learned of the Boston Tea Party, which had taken place on December 16, he informed London that he would not be able to bring the tea ashore without military protection and that it would not be purchased by the colonists. Coincidentally, the Governor's Mansion was destroyed by fire on December 29.

In April 1774, Colden wrote the Earl of Dartmouth, who was secretary of state for the colonies and head of the Board of Trade at the time, his final letter related to Lord Dunmore's suit against him. Colden pointed out that it was the unanimous judgment of

Figure 10. Cadwallader Colden (1688–1776) by Matthew Pratt. Painted in 1771–1772. Courtesy of the Chamber of Commerce, State of New York.

Figure 11. Cadwallader Colden and his grandson, Warren Delancey. Matthew Pratt, painted in 1771–1772. Courtesy of the Metropolitan Museum of Art.

the four judges of the Supreme Court that he had sole right to all the salary and perquisites and emoluments, which he had received. Colden also indicated that he had learned that Dunmore was engaged in efforts to remove him from his position as lieutenant governor.[12] There is no record of an answer.

That year a description of Colden's appearance indicated that "the Governor is the best real Picture of an Old Man that I ever saw. He is 87 years old, has his hearing & sences [sic] as well as ever he had without marks of Age, except in his Eyes which are grown dim & his Head covered with strong white hair. His mind is excellent and he is no churl, indeed he pushed me so hard that I was obliged to shear off."[13]

Tryon departed for England on April 7, 1774, and once again Colden became the acting governor. On April 19, a shipment of tea reached the New York harbor. Three days later, a group dressed as Mohawks boarded the *London* and threw the tea overboard. A second ship bearing tea turned about before anchoring and returned to England. In May the Committee of Fifty One was formed by the Assembly in protest of the Tea Act. That committee became the first public body to suggest a continental Congress.[14] The first Continental Congress met in Carpenter's Hall in Philadelphia from September 5 to October 26, 1774. The eight representatives from New York had specific instructions to pursue a resolution with Great Britain. They did sign the Congress's resolution that prohibited importation from Great Britain. On January 20, 1775, the New York Assembly created a committee to protest the Tea Act. In May a Committee of Sixty, which had replaced the Committee of Fifty One, was, in turn, replaced by the Committee of One Hundred. The members expressed loyalty to the Crown but opposition to parliamentary laws that were established without colonial representation.

While Colden remained in charge of provincial affairs, he received "A Circumstantial Account of an Attack that happened on the 19th of April, 1775" from Thomas Gage, detailing the battle that took place near Lexington, Massachusetts.[15] Colden met with his Council on May 1 consequent to receipt of the information. In response to the Earl of Dartmouth's letter on March 3 calling for compliance on the part of the Assembly and restoration of public tranquility,[16] the Council indicated that the recent acts of hostility precluded any immediate efforts toward reconciliation.[17] The Second Continental Congress convened in Philadelphia on May 10, 1775. Eleven representatives from New York attended. The Congress issued a petition of grievances and right to the king.

On May 18, Colden retired to Spring Hill, never to return

to New York City. On May 27, he wrote to Captain Vandeput of the *Asia*: "When Congress and Committees had taken the entire direction of the Government, it is extremely disagreeable to me to remain a spectator of the Proceedings and confusions in town which I had it not in my power to prevent: I have therefore retired to this place on Long Island where I shall be very happy to see you whenever you can make it agreeable to yourself."[18]

On June 14, the Continental Army was established and, a day later, George Washington was named commander-in-chief. On June 17, the Battle of Bunker Hill energized the colonial movement toward independence. Tryon arrived back in New York on June 25. Ironically, he was obliged to share the city's official welcome on that date with a welcome for George Washington, who was passing through the city en route to Boston. Colden's last published letter on the affairs of the province was addressed to the Earl of Dartmouth on July 3, 1775, informing him that Washington had been appointed commander-in-chief of the Continental Army.[19]

While in retirement at Spring Hill, Colden would have learned that, on July 9, 1776, after the Declaration of Independence was read to Washington's troops at the current site of the New York City Hall, the equestrian statue of King George III was torn down and destroyed. On August 27, at the Battle of Long Island at Brooklyn Heights, on the same island where Colden resided, Washington and the Continental Army were emphatically defeated by British troops. On August 29 and 30, the nine thousand American troops evacuated to Manhattan. Colden died on September 20, 1776, at the age of eighty-eight years and seven months. He was buried in a private cemetery attached to his Spring Hill farm.

೨ *Chapter 8* ൧

EPILOGUE AND LEGACY

Colden affixed his signature to his will on May 20, 1775. It was admitted to probate on March 15, 1779. The will stated that Colden's rights to a sixth part of the minerals and ores in a tract of 1,200 acres of land on the Mohawk River that he formerly held with James Alexander and Lewis Morris and others, and a sixth part of minerals and ores in several tracts of land on the west side of the Catskill Mountains were granted to his grandson Richard Nicolls Colden and his heirs. Colden's son David was to receive Colden's "negro slaves, Horses, Oxen & stock and cattle of all sorts, together with all Carts and Waggons and other implements of Husbandry and likewise all my Household and Table Furniture. . . . I give all my manuscript and printed Books to my son David." Colden excused the debts owed him, by his sons Alexander and Cadwallader provided they made no demands on the estate. The estates' money, bonds, and notes were divided into five parts, equally between his sons Cadwallader and David, and his daughter, Elizabeth Delancey, the children of his deceased son, Alexander, and the children of his deceased daughter, Alice Willet.

Cadwallader, Jr., was heir to the lands at Coldengham; David was the recipient of the lands at Spring Hill, Flushing, Long Island. The remaining lands that Colden owned were to be divided and distributed into the same five equal parts as the money, bonds, and notes. The instructions to the executors were that they divide these allocations as soon as possible, selling some parcels, if necessary to ensure equitable shares. Alice's children were to receive their shares on their twenty-first birthday or on the day of their marriage, whichever came first. Lastly, Colden willed that "my Body be interred in a private manner with as little expense as with common Decency may be." His sons Cadwallader, Jr., and David and his daughter, Elizabeth Delancey, were made executors of the will.[1]

Nothing remains of the Colden Estate at Spring Hill. The farm, which had been leased by Colden on May 12, 1761, from John and Thomas Willet, had been sold to "Lieutenant Governor Cadwallader Colden" on May 12, 1772, for £2,000. Reservation was made in the deed for "a certain *ancient* burying Place, fenced in with a stone fence or stone Ditch (where the family of the Willets have hitherto been interred) to and for the use of the family of said Willets to bury and deposit their dead from henceforth forever."[2]

David Colden, Cadwallader's son who inherited the Spring Hill estate, remained loyal to the Crown during the American Revolution. As a consequence, the property was confiscated in 1779 and purchased on July 30, 1784, by William Conwell of Flushing, Long Island. As the property passed by sale from one owner to the next, the name "Spring Hill" was supplanted by the sequential owners' names. When viewed by Edwin R. Purple in 1873, the house stood on a small elevation on the west side of the farm near the public highway. About one hundred yards northeast of the house, the old cemetery and grave of Cadwallader Colden was located. No sign designated the precise location of Colden's grave.[3]

In 1924, Alexander J. Wall, the librarian of the New York Historical Society, visited the area, and noted that the house was still standing (see fig. 9, on p. 134) and was being used as the office of the Cedar Grove Cemetery. It was known as the "Colden House." The foundations consisted of solid thick walls and the largest of the beams were hand-hewn. The hall and rooms were spacious with high ceilings. There were four chimneys and the doors were hung with H-hinges.[4]

Wall chronicled the history of the Spring Hill homestead. Colden entertained the members of the Council in 1764 and General Gage in 1765 at the house. Soldiers from the artillery often dined there. In 1768, Reverend Samuel Auchmuty, rector of Trinity Church in New York City, visited. Between the time the confiscated estate was sold to William Cromwell in 1784 and April 1804 when it was purchased by the Cedar Grove Cemetery Association, the estate passed through fifteen owners.[5]

The Coldengham estate, like Spring Hill, no longer exists. In 1767, Cadwallader transferred the property to his son, Cadwallader, Jr. A live descendant of the Colden's possesses a manuscript tracing of an original map of the estate (fig. 12). The tracing was made January 4, 1811. The map's written legend indicates that it is "A Map of Coldenham comprehending 2000 acres granted in the year 1719 by Letters Patent To Cadwallader Colden Esq. . . . Also 1000 acres of Land . . . released by his Excellency Gov.[r] Burnet to the said Cadwallader Colden by Indenture bearing the date 9th day of April 1728 . . . and also 720 acres of Land granted by letters Patent to Cadw.[ld] Colden Jun.[r] & David Colden in the year 1761." The map depicts plots allocated to Cadwallader's children: Alexander, Cadwallader, Jr, and Alice Colden, and others. It also indicated areas that had been sold off.

The house in which Cadwallader Colden and his family lived for four decades, was replaced by a stone mansion by Cadwallader, Jr. Over the centuries, the elegant structure gradually disintegrated. The remaining stone elements at the junction of Route 17K and Stone Castle Road between the town of Montgomery and the city of Newburgh, New York, are identified by a sign that reads "SITE OF COLDEN MANSION/ BUILT OF STONE IN 1767/ BY CADWALLADER COLDEN JR./ ESTATE ESTABLISHED IN 1727/ AREA SINCE, COLDENHAM." In the vicinity, in front of the elementary school, another historical marker was erected in 1998. It states, "JANE COLDEN/ 1724–

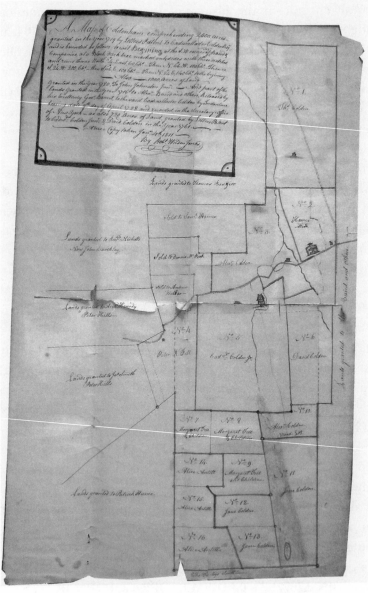

Figure 12. A map of Coldengham, January 4, 1811, designating the segments allocated to Cadwallader Colden's children, Alexander, Cadwallader, Jr., Jane, Alice, Catherine, and David. Courtesy of Robin Assenza, a living relative.

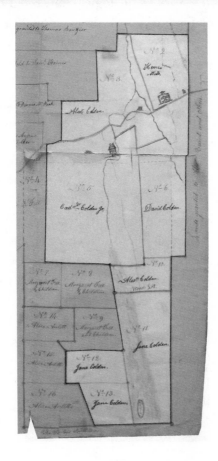

1766. BOTANIST. HER/ RESEARCH, ILLUSTRATIONS AND/ MANUSCRIPT AT THE BRITISH/ MUSEUM ARE INVALUABLE TO HORTICULTURISTS TODAY."

The reconstruction of the stone mansion, which has received National Historical Landmark status, is currently an issue of contention. In Montgomery, the Coldengham Preservation & Historical Society, which consists of about twenty-five members, meets monthly on Sundays. The members are dedicated to sustaining a remembrance of the estate.

The family of Cadwallader and Alice Colden has been the subject of two genealogical works. In 1873, Edwin R. Purple, a member of the New York Genealogical and Biographical Society, had an edition of fifty copies of *Genealogical Notes of The Colden Family in America* privately printed. Recently, The Coldengham Preservation & Historical Society published online an updated genealogy of the family (www.coldenpreservation.org).

Alexander, known familiarly as Sandy, the oldest of the Colden children, was born on August 13, 1716, in Philadelphia. He married Elizabeth, the second daughter of Richard Nicholls of New York City. Nicholls was a distant relative of a seventeenth-century governor of the province of New York. Alexander was appointed ranger of Ulster County in 1737. At an early age, he operated a store in the area of Coldengham. Within six years, he expanded to ownership of a store in Newburgh, a wharf on the Hudson River, a fleet of sailing ships, and a mill on Quassaick Creek. He operated the first ferry from Newburgh to New York City and a ferry to Fishkill across the Hudson River. He accumulated great wealth. Following the solicitation of Governor Clinton by Cadwallader,[6] in 1751, Alexander was appointed joint surveyor general of New York, and he became acting surveyor general when his father became lieutenant governor in 1761. He also became postmaster of New York and a vestryman of Trinity Church. In 1773, he resigned his office of surveyor and searcher of New York in favor of his son,

Nicholls.[7] Alexander died on December 12, 1774; his wife had died at Spring Hill nine months previously. Both were buried in the family vault in the courtyard of Trinity Church. Two of their sons and three of their sons-in-law served with the British Forces during the American Revolution. A grandson, Richard Nicholls's son, was editor of the *U.S. Sporting Magazine* from 1835 to 1836.

The Colden's second child, who was named David, died in infancy. Their first daughter, Elizabeth, was born in New York City on February 5, 1719. On January 7, 1738, she married Peter, third son of Stephen and Ann (Van Cortland) Delancey. Peter owned an extensive estate, and represented the borough of Westchester in the New York Colonial Assembly from 1750 to 1768. Peter died on October 17, 1770. Elizabeth died in 1784. They had twelve children.

The Delancey's oldest son, Stephen, became clerk of the city and county of Albany in 1765. After the war, Stephen's family moved to Quebec. The Delancey's second son, John, represented Westchester in the New York Assembly from 1768 to 1775, when he was elected to the Provincial Congress. A third son, Peter, was a collector under the Stamp Act, but resigned under pressure from the Sons of Liberty. He was killed in a duel on August 16, 1771, in Charleston, South Carolina, by an eminent local physician, Dr. John Haley. The oldest Delancey daughter, Ann, married John Cox of Philadelphia, and had no children. Her younger sister, Alice, to whom along with Ann, Cadwallader had offered advice,[8] married Henry Izard of South Carolina on April 27, 1767. After living in France during the American Revolution, the family returned to America, and Mr. Izard served as a delegate from South Carolina to Congress from 1780 to 1783. He next served as a senator from that state from 1789 to 1795, and, for a brief period, was president of the Senate. One of the Izard children, George, became a major general in the Army, aide-de-camp to Alexander Hamilton, and, later, governor of the Arkansas Territory. Another of the Izard's sons, Ralph, was a naval hero at Tripoli during the first Barbary War. A World War II ship was named in his honor.

Another of the Delancey sons, James, was high sheriff of Westchester County until the Revolutionary War began. He became a colonel in the British forces, and, after the war, moved to Nova Scotia, where he became a member of the council. His younger brother, Oliver, was an officer in the British Navy, but resigned his commission. He continued to live in Westchester, where he died. The youngest son, Warren (see fig. 11, p. 154), distinguished himself while fighting for the British at the Battle of White Plains as a fifteen year old, and was made a coronet. After the war, he continued to reside in Westchester.

Another of the Delanceys' daughters, Suzanna, married Thomas H. Barclay, a New York City lawyer, on October 2, 1775. He joined the British Army as a captain. After the war, he moved to Nova Scotia, where he became speaker of the Provincial Assembly. In 1796, he was appointed commissioner of the province. Suzanna's younger sister, Jane, married James Watt, Jr., also on October 2, 1775. Watt became one of New York's leading citizens, serving in the State Assembly from 1791 to 1793 and as speaker from 1792 to 1795. He also represented New York in Congress from 1792 to 1795

Cadwallader, Jr. (Cad), was born in New York City on May 26, 1722. When he was seven years old, Coldengham became his permanent home. In time, the management of the estate became his responsibility. In 1746, he married Elizabeth, daughter of Thomas Ellison of New Windsor, New York. He occasionally acted as a deputy surveyor for his father. In 1747, he was appointed commissary of the musters by Governor Clinton for his region. Throughout the conflict with the French, Cadwallader, Jr., was an active member of the local militia. He remained a participant until 1775 and rose to the rank of colonel. In 1767, the Coldengham estate was deeded to him by his father, and shortly thereafter he built the stone Colden Mansion. The furniture from one of the rooms is on display at the Metropolitan Museum of Art. In 1768, he was elected first superintendent of Hanover Precinct, now the town of Montgomery. At the onset of the Revolutionary War, as an outspoken loyalist, he was arrested and spent a brief time in jail. He was never formally charged and none of his property was confiscated.

Cadwallader, Jr., and Elizabeth had nine children; two of their sons died in infancy. His four sons, Cadwallader, III, Thomas, Alexander, and David remained in the region of Coldengham and were farmers. Cadwallader, III, was born in 1745. Thomas, was born a year later and died in 1826. He became sheriff of Ulster County in 1774, and served as a captain in the British service during the war. Cadwallader, III, and his brother Alexander, who was born in 1757 and died in 1845, vehemently opposed their father's view and served in the militia in support of the revolution during the war. The youngest son, David, was born in 1762 and did not participate in the war. He inherited part of the estate and also became a respectable farmer. The older daughter, Alice, was born in 1746. She married Dr. Lewis Antill on November 30, 1771. They had two daughters who were raised by her parents after she died in 1776. Alice's younger sister, Jane, lived at home until her father died, after which she married Alexander Murray when she was forty-eight. Cadwallader, Jr., died on February 18, 1797, and is buried in the Colden cemetery on the estate. Elizabeth Colden died in 1815.

Cadwallader Colden's daughter Jane previously has been considered in detail. Her younger sister, Alice, was born in New York City on September 27, 1725. She became the second wife of Colonel William Willet and gave birth to four children, one of whom died in infancy. The Willets' younger daughter, Alice, married Thomas Colden, Cadwallader, Jr.'s son and, therefore, her uncle.

David Colden, the youngest child of Cadwallader and Ann Colden, was born November 23, 1733. At age fourteen, he was afflicted with severe scoliosis which limited his physical activities. In 1761, he moved to his father's farm at Spring Hill and served as Cadwallader's personal secretary. In 1767, David married Ann Willet, the daughter of his Flushing, Long Island, neighbor, on February 27, 1767. In 1775, he succeeded his brother Alexander as surveyor general. David inherited the Spring Hill estate. In 1784, he went to England to gain compensation for the loss of his property that was confiscated at the end of the war. He died in England on July 10, 1784, and was buried at St. Anne's Church, Westminster, where a monument was erected in his honor. His wife died at Coldengham in August 1785.

David was the most intellectually curious of Cadwallader's children. In 1755, his father wrote to his London correspondent Collinson, "I am most concerned for my youngest son David because he is of a weak constitution of body & thereby unfit for any business which requires strength of body & fatigue, tho' at the same time is superior to any of my other children in his intellectual faculties. . . ."[9] David's major scientific interest was electricity, and he was a staunch defender of Franklin's theory of electrical polarity. David conducted his own experiments and defended Franklin's theory against the scientifically revered Abbé Nollet, who had cast doubt on Franklin's experiments and conclusions. The respect that David enjoyed as a scientist is evidenced by the fact that Nollet sent one copy of his own works to Franklin and another to David by way of Franklin. Franklin wrote Cadwallader from London on December 3, 1760, "He [Nollet] sent me a Copy, and another for your Son Mr David Colden. I take the Freedom of forwarding it under your Cover, with my best Respects to that very ingenious young Gentleman, whose valuable Work on the same Subject I am Sorry has not yet been made publick."[10] David's paper was probably published in 1759 in the History of the Academy of Science at Paris.[11]

David and Ann Colden had nine children, five of whom reached adulthood. The most distinguished was Cadwallader David

Colden, who was born at Spring Hill on April 4, 1769. He studied and practiced law. In 1798, he was appointed district attorney of New York. After an illness, he was reappointed in 1810 and served for one year. He was given the rank of colonel at the time of the War of 1812, during which he directed the fortification of New York City. In 1818, he was elected to the Assembly and that year he became mayor of the city. In 1822, he was elected to Congress and, in 1824, to the State Senate. He prepared an elaborate book, which commemorated the opening of the Erie Canal in 1825.[12]

The names of Cadwallader Colden and his grandson Cadwallader David Colden were among the fifteen names on an engraving (fig. 13), which recognized those who played a role in the development of the Erie Canal.

Cadwallader's name headed the list, above that of George Washington, because a century earlier he had proposed a canal across the Iroquois lands. It is ironic that the name of the most reviled political leader in the colonies would preempt that of the name of the most revered person of the time. On the other hand, it was not unreasonable to recognize Cadwallader Colden, who sustained leadership roles for a period of time unmatched by any other individual in the colony, which would become one of thirteen original states, at a time when the opening of a waterway would initiate the transformation of that state. The Erie Canal was the major factor in the evolution of New York City into the commercial capital of the United States and the state's designation as "The Empire State."

In October 1852, Frances Colden, the wife of the great-grandson of Cadwallader Colden, Sr., presented the Colden papers to the New York Historical Society.

An assessment of Colden's legacy is challenging because of the multiple facets of his long life and diverse interests, which merit incorporation in a summation. Among the elements to be evaluated are: his role as a family man, his relationships with friends and

Figure 13. "Early Canal Advocates," an engraving celebrating the 1825 opening of the Erie Canal. From David Hosack. *Memoir of De Witt Clinton; with an appendix, containing numerous documents, illustrative of the principal events of his life.* J. Seymour, New York, 1829. Cadwallader Colden's portrait is at the top of a group of fifteen men who were regarded to be contributory to the development and building of the canal. His grandson, Cadwallader David, is at the bottom of the group represented.

associates, his medical contributions, his inventions, his stature as a cartographer and historian, his esteem as a botanist, his reputation as a philosopher and scientist, his aptitude as a politician, and his effectiveness as a colonial executive and leader.

Cadwallader Colden, as *pater familias*, was beyond reproach and his record as a husband, father, and grandparent is praiseworthy. Cadwallader and Alice Colden enjoyed a mutually satisfying marital relationship of more than forty-six years. Each participated in the social and intellectual development of a large number of children who survived beyond infancy. Among their extensive correspondence, a consequence of Cadwallader's frequent and prolonged absences, there is a persistent pattern of support and concern for each other.

There is no evidence of friction between Colden and his children as they were growing up. Samuel Bard, who joined the household briefly as a child, later expressed appreciation for Colden's guidance. It is apparent from the correspondence that, after the Colden's children left the home, Cadwallader maintained a concern for each of them, and exerted efforts to further their careers and financial security. His familial involvement extended into the next generation as he comfortably offered his grandchildren advice about their education and comportment.

A casual acquaintance pointed out that Colden "had no close friends but a few personal ones, and no enemies but a few public ones."[13] James Alexander stands out as the closest of his colleagues. Most of Colden's persistent personal relationships were epistolary and, rarely, was there any expressed sentimentality. A Scottish authoress, who met him when she was a young girl and described Colden as "of short stature and squared shoulders," wrote in her memoirs that he neither sought to be feared nor loved, but merely to be esteemed and trusted.[14] By contrast, those who visited Coldengham, including, the Bartrams, Alexander Garden, and Peter Kalm, indicated that he was a most congenial host and this attribute continued into his later years at Spring Hill when he entertained.

Colden left no legacy in the realm of medicine. Although he was among the earliest of university trained physicians in the American colonies, he made only a vain attempt to practice his profession during his early days in Philadelphia. In New York he made no attempt at a medical presence. Despite this detachment, Colden maintained an interest in medicine. He continued to purchase and read medical works and contributed to the literature on diverse issues. Although his *Treatise on Wounds and Fevers* continued to be referred to for a while, his writings were admittedly and obviously those of a dilettante. He can be credited with initiating the first public health measures and regulations for the practice of medicine in the colonies.

Colden's attempts at invention came to naught. The quadrant, to which he applied the mechanism and precision of the screw in order to improve surveying, could not "answer expectation when reduced to practice."[15] Colden's conception of the process of stereotyping as a technique for printing was deemed to have little practicality, and, although Colden had no knowledge of it, had been proposed previously in Europe.

Colden's one venture into cartography, over and above the fact that it was the first map to be printed in New York, is of significance. It provides the first graphic representation of the locations of each of the five nations of the Iroquois confederation and depicts multiple places of portage. It also placed several forts, which had been recently established and would become critical during the French and Indian War, on the map for the first time.

By contrast, *The History of the Five Indian Nations*, the most widely read of Colden's narratives, added no new knowledge. It is, in essence, an extrapolation of previous published books. Colden's intimate association with several of the tribes and the personal knowledge that he gained during his surveys throughout the region is unfortunately not expressed. Although the book has been identified as "an important part of the corpus of colonial literature,"[16] it provided no new information or interpretation.

Colden's name was permanently engrained in the annals of botany by Linnaeus, who designated a specific genus *Coldenia* in 1753. Colden merits recognition as the first to introduce Linnaean floral taxonomy in the North American colonies. But once he developed an interest in Newtonian science and, particularly, gravity, he passed the botanical baton on to his daughter Jane in the early 1740s. For the last three decades of his life there is no evidence of his interest in the field in which he had been so intimately involved.

Riley included Colden in his compendium of *American Philosophy; The Early Schools*, and referred to him as "the first and foremost of the early American materialists."[17] Others considered Colden to be "a downright materialist in philosophical conviction"[18] and "the only important American materialist of the eighteenth century prior to the Revolution."[19] However, as a corpus, Colden's printed works were regarded by a critic to be "of no Philosophical concern."[20] Colden's philosophical contributions were merely an incidental byproduct of his attempt to expand Newtonian science and explain the cause of gravity. Colden's unpublished manuscript, "The First Principles of Morality," preceded his "scientific contributions" and regarded the body as machine whose actions are effected by man, and pleasure was a final goal.

His attempts to expand Newton's contributions to physics, optics, and, most critically for Colden, to provide an explanation for the cause of gravitation, were purely literal expressions, devoid of mathematical references and equations. His words presented what was considered to be philosophical ruminations on matter, which he considered to be active and unintelligent, and mind, which he proposed as being extended, active, and intelligent. Colden was a Deist, but the Diety or Spirit did not nor could it act in opposition to the actions of material beings. Colden's writings along these lines were diffuse and his "philosophy" is now rarely invoked.

Colden's appellation of "the most learned man in the Colonies"[21] and Franklin's deference to Colden's knowledge[22] was based mainly on Colden's ventures into Newtonian science. There is no question that Colden had little expertise in mathematics or physics, and no understanding on Newton's concepts. As the justifiable criticism from the most highly regarded mathematicians of the time indicated, Colden's interpretations and proposals were "absurd!"[23] For anyone with less self-assurance, this would have been an embarrassment. But his dogmatism and perseverance remained unfettered.

To Colden's credit, throughout his political career, he never wavered from his oath to serve the king, the Crown, and the laws enacted by the Parliament. At the beginning of his political career, he emerged as a polarizing personality. His most outspoken opponent described Colden as "quick and subtle, conceited and fond of Disputation, easily flattered, and anxious for preeminence in all Topics of Conversation, and rather disgustful than insinuating for he was hot, coarse & assuming." The descriptive nouns assigned to Colden were, "Duplicity, Pride, Craft, Obstinacy, Vanity, Petulance, Ambition, vindictive Spirit and Avarice."[24]

More analytic and less biased evaluations of Colden's political activities ascribed to him a naivety and a lack of tact. He stood out in New York as the figure who bore the most responsibility for endorsing royal authority. A modern historian wrote, "It would not be unfair to call him an unwitting provocateur of the early revolutionary movement in New York."[25]

Almost fifty years after his death, a brief biographical memoir of Cadwallader Colden appeared. In a most complimentary fashion the author pointed out: "Among those to whom this country is most deeply indebted for much of its science, and for very many of its most important institutions, Lieutenant-Governour Colden is very conspicuous; and it is much to be regretted that as yet we have no more ample detail of his character, studies, and public services, than is contained in a brief memoir in a medical journal, and a meager article of a biographical dictionary. . . . With all this propensity to abstract speculation he was remarkable for his habits of dexterity in business and attention to the affairs of ordinary life. A mind thus powerful and active could not have failed to produce great effect on the character of that society in which he moved; and we doubtless enjoy many beneficial, although remote effects of his labours, without being able to trace them to their true source."[26]

The same anonymous writer opined in another journal: "When it is considered how large a portion of his life was spent in the labours or the routine of public office, and that, however great might have been his original stock of learning, he had, in this country, no reading public to excite him by their applauses, and a few literary friends to assist or stimulate his inquiries, his zeal and success in his scientific pursuits will appear deserving of the highest admiration."[27]

More recently, two graduate students were more critical. One biographer notes that "the moment he touched politics . . . his sympathy, his plasticity, his humanity even, dropped from him and he became a martinet, an intolerant theorist, an implacable stickler for the letter of the law, while tact and common sense became qualities to him unknown."[28] The other scholar determined that Colden failed "to perceive the temper of the times" and provided evidence that age intensified his antagonistic and adversarial nature. As one of Colden's contemporaries stated, "the Old Gentleman, tho Eighty-five years old, does not dislike a little controversy, which he has been engaged in for the greatest part of his life."[29]

What would Colden think today if he had the opportunity for retrospective analysis of his life and the ensuing years? For Colden, the consistent and dedicated loyalist, the outcome of the

American Revolution would represent a severe disappointment. The disappearance of his estates at Coldengham and Spring Hill would evoke sadness. Some pleasure would be generated by the course and accomplishments of members of subsequent generations of his family. Particular pleasure would be afforded by the political contributions of his grandson, Cadwallader David. In that regard, the development of the Erie Canal, as evidence of the practicality of his early visionary proposal, would provide personal satisfaction.

Cadwallader Colden would question whether his contemporaries and subsequent critics were prejudiced in their focus on his frailties, his political problems, and his intellectual inadequacies. He would be devastated to learn that Benjamin Franklin, his intellectual compatriot, did not mention him in an autobiography, which was started while Colden was still alive. His ego would gain satisfaction with the nine volumes of his correspondence and notes that the New York Historical Society published. But this would be offset by the realization that his life and contribution excited the scholarly interest of only two historians, and that the two scholars' concern with him was a vehicle to satisfy the requirements for a graduate degree. Finally, almost 240 years after his death, he could have to evaluate whether this, the first formal biography of him, was appropriately balanced.

ᕇ ENDNOTES ᕒ

INTRODUCTION

1. Alice Mapelsden Keys, *Cadwallader Colden: A Representative Eighteenth Century Official* (New York: self-published), 1906.

2. Alfred R. Hoermann, *Cadwallader Colden: A Figure of the American Enlightenment* (Westport, CT: Green Press, 2002).

CHAPTER 1: BEFORE TAKING ROOT: 1688–1718

a. This is in accordance with The New York Historical Papers. The *American National Biography* lists the date as February 7, 1689; the *Dictionary of National Biography* indicates the date to be February 17, 1688; the *Genealogical Notes of the Colden Family in America* by Edwin R. Purple, privately printed in New York in 1873, offers a date of February 7, 1687, O.S.

1. *American National Biography* Vol. 5 (Oxford and New York: Oxford University Press, 1999), pp. 198–99.

2. *The Letters and Papers of Cadwallader Colden*, Vol. II, Collections of The New York Historical Society for the Year 1918, New York, pp. 72–80.

3. Alfred R. Hoermann, *Cadwallader Colden: A Figure of the American Enlightenment* (Westport, CT: Greenwood Press, 2003), p. 76.

4. Alexander Grant, *The Story of the University of Edinburgh*, Vol. 1 (London: Longmans, Green, 1884), p. 220.

5. *The Letters and Papers of Cadwallader Colden*, Vol. IV, Collections of the New York Historical Society for the Year 1920, New York, p. 258.

6. Ibid.

7. Ibid., p. 259.

8. *The Letters and Papers of Cadwallader Colden*, Vol. I, Collections of the New York Historical Society for the Year 1918, New York, p. 39.

9. *The Letters and Papers of Cadwallader Colden*, Vol. II, pp. 126–27.

10. *Dictionary of National Biography*, Vol. 4 (Oxford: Oxford University Press, 1964), p. 716.

11. *The Letters and Papers of Cadwallader Colden*, Vol. I, p. 34.

12. Ibid., pp. 41–42.

13. Ibid., pp. 37–39.

14. William Smith, Jr., *The History of the Province of New-York . . . to the Year MDCCXXXII* (London, 1757), Vol. I, Michael Kammen, ed., (Cambridge, MA: The Belknap Press of Harvard University Press, 1972), p. 212.

15. Joseph M. Toner, *Contributions to the Annals of Medical Progress and medical education in the United States before and during the war of independence* (Washington, DC: Government Printing Office, 1874), p. 106.

16. William Douglass, *A Summary, Historical and Political, of the . . . British Settlements in North-America*, 2 vols. (London: R. and J. Dodsley, 1760), p. 106.

17. Richard Harrison Shryock, *Medicine and Society in America 1660-1680* (New York: New York University Press, 1972), p. 9.

18. S. Griffin to Levi Bartlett [April 4, 1794], Miller Collection, Richmond, VA. Academy of Medicine.

19. Francis R. Packard, *History of Medicine in the United States*, Vol. 1, (New York: Paul B. Hoeber, 1931), p. 286.

20. Frederick B. Tolles, *James Logan and the Culture of Provincial America* (Boston: Little, Brown and Co., 1957), p. 6.

21. Ibid.

22. Ibid.

CHAPTER 2: THE NEW NEW YORKER: 1718-1728

a. It was customary to designate two years, one representing the old style and the other the new style calendar. In 1750, an Act of Parliament changed the calendar so that the new year began on January 1 rather than March 25 and would run according to the Gregorian calendar. The new calendar took effect on January 1, 1752.

1. Seymour I. Schwartz and Ralph E. Ehrenberg, *The Mapping of America* (New York: Harry N. Abrams, 1980), pp. 75–79.

2. Michael Kammen, *Colonial New York-A History* (New York: Charles Scriber's Sons, 1975), p. 180.

3. Edwin R. Purple, *Genealogical Notes on the Colden Family* (Private printing, 1873).

4. Ibid.

5. Alice Mapelsden Keys, *Cadwallader Colden: A Representative Eighteenth Century Official* (New York: n.p., 1906), p. 27.

6. *The Letters and Papers of Cadwallader Colden*, Vol. IV, Collections of the New York Historical Society for the Year 1917, New York, p. 100–101.

7. Keys, *Cadwallader Colden*, p. 108.

8. William Smith, Jr., *The History of the Province of New-York . . . to the Year MDCCXXXII*, London, 1757, Vol. I, Michael Kammen, ed. (Cambridge, MA: The Belknap Press of Harvard University Press, 1972), p. 16.

9. Francis R. Packard, *History of Medicine in the United States*, Vol. I (New York: Paul B. Hoeber, 1931), p. 297.

10. Cadwallader Colden, "To His Excellency Brigadier Hunter Governor of New York, January 16, 1719/20," *Copy Book of Letters on Subjects of Philosophy, Medicine, Friendship, 1716-1721*, Colden MS., New York Historical Society, unpaginated.

11. Ibid.

12. *The Letters and Papers of Cadwallader Colden*, Vol. I, Collections of the New York Historical Society for the Year 1917, New York, pp. 114–23.

13. Ibid., pp. 141–45.

14. Ibid., p. 164.

15. Ibid., pp. 165–67.

16. Ibid., pp. 234–37, 244, 246, 247.

17. Ibid., pp. 238–39, 244–45.

18. Ibid., pp. 244, 245, 247, 250–51.

19. Charles J. Bullock, "Introduction: Life and Writings of William

Douglass," in "A Discourse Concerning the Currencies of the British Plantations in America &c. by William Douglass," ed. by Charles J. Bullock, *Economic Studies* (*Journal of the American Economic Association*), Vol. 2, No. 5, Google Books.

20. *The Letters and Papers of Cadwallader Colden*, Vol. I, pp. 272–73.

21. *The Letters and Papers of Cadwallader Colden*, Vol. II, Collections of the New York Historical Society for the Year 1918, New York, pp. 146–47.

22. Ibid., pp. 196–200.

23. Seymour I. Schwartz and Ralph E. Ehrenberg, *The Mapping of America* (New York: Harry N. Abrams, 1980), p. 157.

24. Keys, *Cadwallader Colden*, p. 29.

25. Ibid., p. 31.

26. Shelley Ross, *Fall From Grace* (New York: Random House, 1958), p. 4.

27. Keys, *Cadwallader Colden* p. 31.

28. *The Letters and Papers of Cadwallader Colden*, Vol. I, pp. 104–105.

29. Alphonso T. Clearwater, ed., *The History of Ulster County New York* (Westminster, MD: Clearwater, Heritage Book Facsimile, 2007), p. 53.

30. Keys, *Cadwallader Colden*, p. 33.

31. *The Letters and Papers of Cadwallader Colden*, Vol. I, pp. 128–34.

32. Schwartz and Ehrenberg, *The Mapping of America*, p. 150.

33. Baron de Lahontan, *Nouveaux Voyages de Mr. Baron de Lahontan Dans L'Amerique Septentrionale* (La Haye: Chez les Freres l Honore, 1702).

34. Ibid., p. 146.

35. *The Letters and Papers of Cadwallader Colden*, Vol. I, 1919, p. 209.

36. Keys, *Cadwallader Colden*, p. 5.

37. John Huske, *The Present State of North America* (London: R. and J. Dodsley, 1755), pp. 41-42.

38. Smith, *The History of the Province of New-York*, Vol. I, p. lxiii.

39. Lawrence C. Wroth, *An American Bookshelf 1755* (Philadelphia: University of Pennsylvania Press, 1934).

40. Cadwallader Colden, *The History of the Five Indian Nations* (New York: William Bradford, 1727; Ithaca and London: Cornell University Press, 1973), p. ix.

41. *Histoire de L'Amerique septentrionale pr Mr. de Bacqueville de la Potherie* (Paris: J. L. Nion et F. Didot, 1722).

42. Baron de Lahontan, *Nouveaux Voyages de Mr.Baron de Lahontan Dans L'Amerique Septentrionale.*

43. Colden, *The History of the Five Indian Nations.*

44. Keys, *Cadwallader Colden*, p. 112.

45. Edwin R. Purple, *Genealogical Notes on the Colden Family* (Private printing, 1873), p. 4.

46. Edmund B. O'Callaghan, ed., *Documents Relative to the Colonial History of New York*, Vol. V (Albany, 1856–87), pp. 685–88.

47. William Smith, Jr., *The History of the Province of New-York*, Vol. I, p. 172.

48. Edwin R. Purple, *Genealogical Notes on the Colden Family*, p. 8.

49. Smith, *The History of the Province of New-York*, Vol. I, p. 171.

50. Michael Kammen, *Colonial New York-A History*, pp. 184–85.

51. *The Letters and Papers of Cadwallader Colden*, Vol. IX, Collections of the New York Historical Society for the Year 1937, New York, p. 278.

52. *The Letters and Papers of Cadwallader Colden*, Vol. I, pp. 191–92.

53. Jean O'Neill and Elizabeth P. McLean, *Petyer Collinson and the Eighteenth-Century Natural History Exchange* (Philadelphia: American Philosophical Society, 2008).

54. Smith, *The History of the Province of New-York*, Vol. I, p. 318.

55. *The Letters and Papers of Cadwallader Colden*, Vol. II, p. 263.

56. Jacquetta M. Haley, "Farming on the Hudson Valley Frontier: Cadwallader Colden's Farm Journal, 1717–1736," *Hudson Valley Regional Review* 6 (March 1989), p. 2.

57. *The Letters and Papers of Cadwallader Colden*, Vol. VIII, Collections of the New York Historical Society for the Year 1934, New York, p. 173.

58. Haley, "Farming on the Hudson Valley Frontier," p. 6.

59. Ibid., pp. 1–34.

60. Paula Ivaska Robbins, *Jane Colden: America's First Woman Botanist* (New York: Purple Mountain Press, Fleischmanns, 2009), p. 22.

61. Ibid.

62. *The Letters and Papers of Cadwallader Colden*, Vol. I, p. 274.

63. Ibid., pp. 271–72.

CHAPTER 3: A COUNTRY GENTLEMAN REMAINS FOCUSED ON COLONIAL CONCERNS: 1729–1738

1. *The Letters and Papers of Cadwallader Colden,* Vol. II, Collections of the New York Historical Society for the Year 1917, New York, p. 6.

2. Ibid., p. 84.

3. *The Letters and Papers of Cadwallader Colden,* Vol. VIII, Collections of the New York Historical Society for the Year 1934, New York, p. 202.

4. Jacquetta M. Haley, "Farming on the Hudson Valley Frontier: Cadwallader Colden's Farm Journal, 1717–1736," *Hudson Valley Regional Review* 6 (March 1989), p. 6.

5. Paula Ivaska Robbins, *Jane Colden: America's First Woman Botanist* (New York: Purple Mountain Press, Fleischmanns, 2009), p. 24.

6. Haley, "Farming on the Hudson Valley Frontier," p. 6.

7. Ibid., p. 4.

8. Ibid., pp. 1–34.

9. Joseph Devine, "Cadwallader Colden: Father of the American Canal System." http://home.roadrunner.com/-montghistory/ (accessed 2012).

10. Cadwallader Colden, "Observations on the Situation, Soil, Climate, Water, Communications, Bounaries, etc. of the Province of New York, (1738)" in E. B. O'Callaghan, *The Documentary History of the State of New York* (Albany, NY: State of New York, 1849–1851), Vol. I, pp. 172–73.

11. *The Letters and Papers of Cadwallader Colden,* Vol. VIII, pp. 198 and 200.

12. Alice Colden Wadsworth, "Sketch of the Colden and Murray Families" (1819), Manuscript Division, New York Public Library, quoted in Alfred R. Hoermann, *Cadwallader Colden; A Figure of the American Enlightmenment* (Westport, CT: Greenwood Press, 2002), p. 17.

13. *The Letters and Papers of Cadwallader Colden,* Vol. II, p. 180.

14. Ibid., pp. 146–47.

15. William Smith, Jr., *The History of the Province of New-York . . . to the Year MDCCXXXII* (London, 1757, Vol. I), Michael Kammen, ed., (Cambridge, MA: The Belknap Press of Harvard University Press, 1972) p. 187.

16. Ibid., p. 188.

17. Alice Mapelsden Keys, *Cadwallader Colden: A Representative Eighteenth Century Official* (New York: 1906), p. 51.

18. *The Letters and Papers of Cadwallader Colden*, Vol. II, pp. 124–28.

19. Keys, *Cadwallader Colden*, p. 39.

20. Ibid., p. 41.

21. *The Letters and Papers of Cadwallader Colden*, Vol. II, pp. 172–75.

22. Ibid., p. 205.

23. Ibid., p. 102.

24. Ibid., p. 115.

25. Smith, *The History of the Province of New-York . . . to the Year MDCCXXXII*, p. 15.

26. Ibid., p. 21.

27. *The Letters and Papers of Cadwallader Colden*, Vol. II, p. 141.

28. Michael Kammen, *Colonial New York-A History* (New York: Charles Scriber's Sons, 1975), pp. 203–205.

29. Ibid., p. 28.

30. *The Letters and Papers of Cadwallader Colden*, Vol. II, pp. 158–60.

31. Smith, *The History of the Province of New-York . . . to the Year MDCCXXXII*, pp. 33–35.

32. Ibid., p. lxxi.

33. Ibid., p. 195.

34. Ibid., p. lxx.

CHAPTER 4: CONCENTRATED CORRESPONDENCE AND EVOLVING ENLIGHTENMENT:
1739–1748

1. *The Letters and Papers of Cadwallader Colden*, Vol. II, Collections of the Historical Society for the Year 1917, New York, p. 210.

2. *The Letters and Papers of Cadwallader Colden*, Vol. VIII, Collections of the Historical Society for the Year 1937, New York, p. 355.

3. *The Letters and Papers of Cadwallader Colden*, Vol. II, p. 205.

4. Ibid., pp. 206–209.

5. Ibid., p. 208.

6. Whitfield J. Bell, Jr., *Patriot Improvers: Biographical Sketches of Members of the American Philosophical Society*, Vol. 1, (Philadelphia: American Philosophical Society, 1997), p. 111.

7. *The Letters and Papers of Cadwallader Colden*, Vol. II, p. 281.

8. *The Letters and Papers of Cadwallader Colden*, Vol., V, Collections of the New-York Historical Society for the Year 1921, New York, p. 216.

9. Ibid., p. 31–33.

10. Edmund Berkeley and Doris Smith Berkeley, *The Correspondence of John Bartram, 1734-1777* (Gainesville: University of Florida Press, 1992), p. 202.

11. Ibid., pp. 86 and 87.

12. "Plantae Coldenghamiae in provincial Novaboracnesi Americes sponte crescents, quas ad Methodem Cl. Linnaei sexulem. Anno 1742 etc. Observavit et descripsit Cadwallader Colden," *Acta Societatis Regiae Scientiarum Upsalinsis* for 1743, 1749, pp. 47–82.

13. *The Letters and Papers of Cadwallader Colden*, Vol. III, Collections of the New York Historical Society for the Year 1919, New York, p. 275.

14. Ibid., p. 38.

15. Ibid. pp. 92–94.

16. Ibid., p. 410.

17. Ibid., p. 34.

18. Ibid., pp. 58–59.

19. Ibid., p. 77.

20. Ibid., pp. 139–43.

21. Ibid., pp. 184 and 185.

22. Ibid., p. 187.

23. Ibid., p. 275.

24. *The Letters and Papers of Cadwallader Colden*, Vol. IV, Collections of the New York Historical Society for the Year 1920, New York, p. 6.

25. "Plantae Coldenghamiae in provincial Novaboracnesi Americes sponte crescents, quas ad Methodem Cl. Linnaei sexulem. Anno 1742 etc. Observavit et descripsit Cadwallader Colden," p. 114.

26. Ibid., p. 34.

27. Brooke Hindle, *The Pursuit of Science in Revolutionary America, 1735-1789* (Chapel Hill: The University of North Carolina Press, 1956), p. 68.

28. Bell, *Patriot Improvers*, pp. 4–6.

29. Hindle, *The Pursuit of Science in Revolutionary America, 1735-1789*, p. 70.

30. *The Letters and Papers of Cadwallader Colden*, Vol. III, p. 143.

31. Ibid., p. 93.

32. Bell, *Patriot Improvers*, p. 111.

33. *The Letters and Papers of Cadwallader Colden*, Vol. III, p. 46.

34. Cadwallader Colden, "Observations on the Fever which prevailed in the City of New-York in 1741 and 2, written in 1743," *American Medical and Philosophical Reporter*, 1 (1811), p. 311.

35. Ibid., p. 589.

36. *The Letters and Papers of Cadwallader Colden*, Vol. III, pp. 65 and 66.

37. Ibid., p. 96.

38. Ibid., p. 102.

39. Ibid., pp. 77 and 78.

40. Ibid., pp. 314–28.

41. Saul Jarcho, "John Mitchell, Benjamin Rush and Yellow Fever," *Bulletin of the History of Medicine*, XXXI (1957), pp. 132–36.

42. Ibid., pp. 328–37.

43. Ibid., p. 236.

44. Bell, *Patriot Improvers*, pp. 138 and 139.

45. Edmund Berkeley and Dorothy Smith Berkeley, *Dr. John Mitchell* (Chapel Hill: The University of North Carolina Press, 1974), p. 24.

46. Herbert Thatcher, "Dr. Mitchell, M.D., F.R.S. of Virginia," *The Virginia Magazine of History and Biography*, 40 (1932), p. 101.

47. D. D. Jo. Mitchell, "Dissertatio Brevis de Principiis Botanicorum et Zoologorum desque novo stabilende naturae rerum congruo cum Appendice Aliquot Generum plantarum recens conditorum . . ." *Acta Physico-Medica Academiae Caesarae . . . Ephemerides VIII*, 1748.

48. Berkeley and Berkeley, *Dr. John Mitchell*, p. 36.

49. Ibid., p. 44.

50. John Mitchell, "An Essay upon the Causes of the Different Colours of People in Different Climates," *Philosophical Transactions*, XLIII (1744), pp. 102–150.

51. Berkeley and Berkeley, *Dr. John Mitchell*, p. 73.

52. *The Letters and Papers of Cadwallader Colden*, Vol. III, p. 369.

184   ENDNOTES

53. Colden to Mitchell, July 6, 1749, *Letters and Papers of Cadwallader Colden*, Vol. IX, Collections of the New York Historical Society for the Year 1937, New York, pp. 18–36.

54. Berkeley and Berkeley, *Dr. John Mitchell*, 1974.

55. Referred to in an inscription on the Mitchell map by John Pownall, secretary to the Board of Trade and Plantations.

56. Seymour I. Schwartz and Ralph E. Ehrenberg, *The Mapping of America* (New York: Harry N. Abrams, 1979), p. 162.

57. Berkeley and Berkeley, *Dr. John Mitchell*, pp. 216–18.

58. Ibid., p. 224.

59. Bell, *Patriot Improvers*, p. 147.

60. Alfred R. Hoermann, *Cadwallader Colden: A Figure of the American Enlightenment* (Westport, CT: Greenwood Press, 2002), p. 77.

61. *The Letters and Papers of Cadwallader Colden*, Vol. III, p. 118.

62. Ibid., p. 212.

63. Sir Isaac Newton, *Mathematical Principles of Natural Philosophy*, ed. by Florian Cajori from the 1737 edition (Berkeley: University of California Press, 1946), p. 547.

64. Raymond Phineas Stearns, *Science in the British Colonies of America* (Urbana: University of Illinois Press, 1970), pp. 568 and 569.

65. Brooke Hindle, "Cadwallader Colden's Extension of the Newtonian Principles," *The William and Mary Quarterly*, Third Series, 13, no. 4 (1956), p. 459.

66. Cadwallader Colden, Manuscript Revision of the *Principles of Action*, Library, University of Edinburgh, ch. 3, p. 37.

67. Ibid., p. 40.

68. Brooke Hindle, "Cadwallader Colden's Extension of the Newtonian Principles," *The William and Mary Quarterly*, Third Series, 13, no. 4 (1956), pp. 464 and 465.

69. *The Letters and Papers of Cadwallader Colden*, Vol. III, p. 6.

70. Ibid., p. 61.

71. Ibid., p. 77.

72. Ibid., p. 1.

73. Ibid., pp. 6–9.

74. I. Woodbridge Riley, *American Philosophy: The Early Schools* (New York: Dodd, Mead & Company, 1907), pp. 323–72.

75. Ibid., pp. 194–96.

76. Ibid., pp. 196 and 224.

77. Ibid., p. 368.

78. Ibid., p. 371.

79. Ibid., p. 331.

80. Ibid., p. 412.

81. *The Letters and Papers of Cadwallader Colden,* Vol. III, pp. 39 and 40.

82. Ibid., p. 127.

83. Ibid., p. 142.

84. Ibid., pp. 282 and 283.

85. Ibid., pp. 207 and 208.

86. Ibid., p. 373.

87. Riley, *American Philosophy: The Early Schools,* p. 338.

88. Max Sevelle, *Seeds of Liberty: The Genesis of the American Mind* (New York: A. A. Knopf, 1948), p. 172.

89. Louis L. Gitlin, "Cadwallader Colden as Scientist and Philosopher," *New York History,* 16 (1935), p. 175.

90. *The Letters and Papers of Cadwallader Colden,* Vol. III, p. 147.

91. Riley, *American Philosophy: The Early Schools,* p. 338.

92. Ibid., p. 341.

93. Hoermann, *Cadwallader Colden: A Figure of the American Enlightenment,* p. 115.

94. Ibid., p. 120.

95. Ibid., p. 117.

96. Ibid., p. 125.

97. Cadwallader Colden, "Of the First Principles of Morality or the Actions of Intelligent Beings," Manuscript I, Rosenbach Museum and Library, Philadelphia.

98. Smith, *The History of the Province of New-York . . . to the Year MDCCXXXII,* p. 44.

99. *The Letters and Papers of Cadwallader Colden,* Vol. III, p. 23.

100. Smith, *The History of the Province of New-York . . . to the Year MDCCXXXII,* pp. 72 and 73.

101. *The Letters and Papers of Cadwallader Colden,* Vol. III, p. 261.

102. Ibid., p. 73.

103. Ibid., p. 353.

104. Ibid., p. 254.

105. Ibid., pp. 284–90.

106. Keys, *Cadwallader Colden: A Representative Eighteenth Century Official*, pp. 155–57.

107. *The Letters and Papers of Cadwallader Colden*, Vol. III, pp. 294–305.

108. Ibid., pp. 339–57.

109. Keys, *Cadwallader Colden: A Representative Eighteenth Century Official*, p. 267.

110. *The Letters and Papers of Cadwallader Colden*, Vol. III, New York, p. 382.

111. Ibid., p. 392.

112. *The Letters and Papers of Cadwallader Colden*, Vol. IX, Collections of the Historical Society for the Year 1937, New York, pp. 359–434.

113. Ibid.

114. *The Letters and Papers of Cadwallader Colden*, Vol. IV, Collections of the Historical Society for the Year 1920, New York, p. 10.

115. Ibid., pp. 24–26.

116. Ibid., pp. 43 and 44.

117. Smith, *The History of the Province of New-York . . . to the Year MDCCXXXII*, p. 113.

118. Keys, *Cadwallader Colden: A Representative Eighteenth Century Official*, pp. 294–96.

119. Martin Kerkhonen, *Peter Kalm's North American Journey: Its Ideological Background and Results* (Helsinki: The Finnish Historical Society, 1959), p. 96.

120. Ibid., pp. 50–60.

121. Ibid., pp. 78 and 79.

CHAPTER 5: CONTINUITY AND CHANGE: 1749–1758

1. *The Letters and Papers of Cadwallader Colden*, Vol. IV, Collections of the Historical Society for the Year 1920, New York, p. 88.

2. Ibid., p. 94.

3. Ibid., p. 109.

4. Ibid. pp. 119–29.

5. Ibid., pp. 159–65.

6. *The Letters and Papers of Cadwallader Colden*, Vol. IX, Collections of the New York Historical Society for the Year 1937, New York, p. 77.

7. *The Letters and Papers of Cadwallader Colden*, Vol. IV, p. 244.

8. *The Letters and Papers of Cadwallader Colden*, Vol. V, Collections of the New-York Historical Society for the Year 1921, New York, p. 13.

9. Ibid., pp. 206 and 207.

10. Ibid., pp. 305 and 306.

11. William Smith, Jr., *The History of the Province of New-York . . . to the Year MDCCXXXII*, London, 1757, Vol. 2, Michael Kammen, ed., (Cambridge, MA: The Belknap Press of Harvard University Press, 1972), p. 123.

12. *The Letters and Papers of Cadwallader Colden*, Vol. IX, pp. 122–24.

13. Ibid., p. 117.

14. Ibid., pp. 95–98.

15. Ibid., p. 101.

16. Edmund Berkeley and Dorothy Smith Berkeley, *Dr. John Mitchell* (Chapel Hill: The University of North Carolina Press, 1974), p. 167.

17. *The Letters and Papers of Cadwallader Colden*, Vol. IV, p. 287.

18. Ibid., pp. 389–91.

19. Smith, *The History of the Province of New-York . . . to the Year MDCCXXXII*, pp. 132–41.

20. Ibid., pp. 142–46.

21. *The Letters and Papers of Cadwallader Colden*, Vol. V, pp. 74, 77, 98, 105–107, 110–11.

22. Smith, *The History of the Province of New-York . . . to the Year MDCCXXXII*, London, 1757, Vol. 2, pp. 201 and 202.

23. *The Letters and Papers of Cadwallader Colden*, Vol. IV, pp. 271–87.

24. Seymour I. Schwartz, *The French and Indian War 1754-1763* (New York, Simon & Schuster, 1994), p. 24.

25. *The Letters and Papers of Cadwallader Colden*. Vol. IV, pp. 449–51.

26. Ibid., pp. 452–57.

27. Smith, *The History of the Province of New-York . . . to the Year MDCCXXXII*, p. 160.

28. Schwartz, *The French and Indian War 1754-1763*, p. 46.

29. *The Letters and Papers of Cadwallader Colden*, Vol. V, p. 18.

30. Schwartz, *The French and Indian War 1754-1763*, p. 81.

31. *The Letters and Papers of Cadwallader Colden*, Vol. V, p. 102.

32. Ibid., pp. 157–67.

33. Ibid., pp. 171–80.

34. Ibid., p. 183.

35. Ibid., pp. 209–211.

36. Ibid., p. 212.

37. Ibid., pp. 249–55.

38. Raymond Phineas Stearns, *Science in the British Colonies of America* (Urbana: University of Illinois Press, 1970), p. 562.

39. *The Letters and Papers of Cadwallader Colden*, Vol. IV, p. 317.

40. Ibid., p. 354.

41. Stearns, *Science in the British Colonies of America*, p. 563.

42. *The Letters and Papers of Cadwallader Colden*, Collections of the New York Historical Society for the Year 1919, New York, p. 44.

43. *The Letters and Papers of Cadwallader Colden*, Vol. IV, p. 64.

44. Ibid., pp. 270–71.

45. Lawrence C. Wroth, *An American Bookshelf 1755*, (Philadelphia: University of Pennsylvania Press, 1934), p. 178.

46. *The Letters and Papers of Cadwallader Colden*, Vol. IV, pp. 206–207.

47. Ibid., pp. 384 and 413.

48. Alfred R. Hoermann, *Cadwallader Colden: A Figure of the American Enlightenment* (Westport, CT: Greenwood Press, 2002), pp. 82–83.

49. *The Letters and Papers of Cadwallader Colden*, Vol. IV, pp. 355–57.

50. Ibid. p. 414.

51. Brooke Hindle, *The Pursuit of Science in Revolutionary America 1735-1789* (Chapel Hill: The University of North Carolina Press, 1956), p. 46.

52. "Criticism of *The Principles of the Action in Matter*," unpublished translation of Kastner's remarks, Colden MSS, New York Historical Society.

53. *The Letters and Papers of Cadwallader Colden*, Vol. IV, p. 473.

54. *The Letters and Papers of Cadwallader Colden*, Vol. IX, pp. 144–48.

55. *The Letters and Papers of Cadwallader Colden*, Vol. V, pp. 22–24.

56. *The Letters and Papers of Cadwallader Colden*, Vol. VI, pp. 197–98.

57. Ibid., p. 273.

58. *The Letters and Papers of Cadwallader Colden*, Vol. IV, pp. 156–58.

59. Ibid., pp. 217 and 218.

60. Ibid., pp. 314–16.

61. Ibid., p. 321.

62. Ibid., pp. 325–27, 337–39.

63. Ibid., p. 353.

64. Ibid., p. 383.

65. Ibid., pp. 421–30.

66. *The Letters and Papers of Cadwallader Colden*, Vol. V, p. 207.

67. *The Letters and Papers of Cadwallader Colden*, Vol. IV, p. 417.

68. Ibid., p. 439.

69. Stearns, *Science in the British Colonies of America*, p. 630.

70. *The Letters and Papers of Cadwallader Colden*, Vol. IV, p. 98.

71. Ibid., p. 251.

72. Ibid., p. 207.

73. Ibid., pp. 258–61.

74. Ibid., p. 471–73.

75. Marcus B. Simpson, Jr., in *American National Biography* (New York and Oxford, University of Oxford Press, 1999), pp. 691–92.

76. Edmund Berkeley and Dorothy Smith Berkeley, *Dr. Alexander Garden of Charles Town* (Chapel Hill: University of North Carolina Press, 1969), p. 42.

77. Stearns, *Science in the British Colonies of America*, p. 601

78. Ibid., pp. 43 and 74.

79. *The Letters and Papers of Cadwallader Colden*, Vol. V, pp. 1–2.

80. Brooke Hindle, *The Pursuit of Science in Revolutionary America 1735-1789* (Chapel Hill: The University of North Carolina Press, 1956), p. 53.

81. Margaret Denny, "Linnaeus and His Disciple in Carolina: Alexander Garden," *Isis*, 38 (1948), p. 173.

82. *The Letters and Papers of Cadwallader Colden*, Vol. VII, Collections of the New York Historical Society for the Year 1923, New York, p. 141.

83. Berkeley and Berkeley, *Dr. Alexander Garden of Charles Town*, p. 216.

84. Garden to Ellis, December 16, 1765, James Edward Smith, ed., *A Selection of the Correspondence of Linnaeus and Other Naturalists*, Vol. I (London: Longman, Hurst, Rees, Orme and Brown, 1821), pp. 543–44.

85. James Britten, "Biographical Notes, VIII—Jan Colden and the Flora of New York," *Journal of Botany, British and Foreign*, 33 (1895), pp. 12–15.

86. Berkeley and Berkeley, *Dr. Alexander Garden of Charles Town*, p. 48.

87. The *Aberdeen Magazine for the Year XDCCLXI*, Aberdeen Scotland, 1761.

88. Berkeley and Berkeley, *Dr. Alexander Garden of Charles Town*, p. 43.

89. *The Letters and Papers of Cadwallader Colden*, Vol. IV, p. 158.

90. Ann Murray Vail, "Jane Colden, An Early New York Botanist," *Torreya*, 7 (1907), p. 32.

91. *The Letters and Papers of Cadwallader Colden*, Vol. V, pp. 29–30.

92. Ibid., p. 37.

93. Ibid., p. 139.

94. W. Darlington, *Memorials of John Bartram and Humphry Marhsall* (Philadelphia, 1849), p. 195.

95. Ibid., p. 202.

96. Ibid., p. 400.

97. John McVickar, *A Domestic Narrative of the Life of Samuel Bard, M.D., LL.D, Late President of the College of Physicians and Surgeons of the University of the State of New York* (New York, 1822), p. 19.

98. Bryon Polk Stookey, *A History of Colonial Medical Education in the Province of New York with Its Subsequent Development* (Springfield, IL: Charles C. Thomas, 1961), pp. 40 and 41.

99. H. W. Rickett and E. C. Hall, eds., *Botanic Manuscript of Jane Colden* (New York: Garden Club of Orange and Dutchess Counties, 1963), p. 53.

100. Britten, "Bibliographical Notes, VIII—Jane Colden and the Flora of New York," p. 15.

101. Rickett and Hall, eds., *Botanic Manuscript of Jane Colden*, p. 23.

102. Ibid., p. 20.

103. Britten, "Bibliographical Notes, VIII—Jane Colden and the Flora of New York," pp. 15–16.

104. Ibid., p. 14.

105. Rickett and Hall, eds., *Botanic Manuscript of Jane Colden*, p. 20.

106. *The Letters and Papers of Cadwallader Colden*, Vol. V, pp. 55–63.

107. Vail, "Jane Colden, An Early New York Botanist," p. 32.

CHAPTER 6: POLITICAL PEAK AND REPUTATIONAL NADIR: 1759–1768

1. *The Letters and Papers of Cadwallader Colden*, Vol. V, Collections of the New-York Historical Society for the Year 1921, New York, 1923, pp. 283–86.

2. Ibid., pp. 289–93.

3. Ibid., pp. 293–95.

4. Ibid., pp. 310–19.

5. Joseph L. Blaue, *Men and Movements in American Philosophy* (New York: Prentice-Hall, 1952), p. 211.

6. William Smith, Jr., *The History of the Province of New-York, Volume Two, A Continuation, 1732–1762*, Michael Kammen, ed., (Cambridge, MA: The Belknap Press, Harvard University Press, 1972), p. 243.

7. Bryon Polk Stookey, *A History of Colonial Medical Education in the Province of New York with Its Subsequent Development* (Springfield, IL: Charles C. Thomas, 1961), pp. 8 and 9.

8. Ibid., p. 247.

9. Ibid., pp. 328 and 329.

10. Ibid., p. 346.

11. Smith, *The History of the Province of New-York, Volume Two, A Continuation, 1732-1762*, p. 251.

12. *The Letters and Papers of Cadwallader Colden*, Vol. V, p. 368.

13. Smith, *The History of the Province of New-York, Volume Two, A Continuation, 1732-1762*, p. 252.

14. Alice Mapelsden Keys, *Cadwallader Colden: A Representative Eighteenth Century Official* (New York, 1906), p. 267.

15. Ibid., p. 269.

16. Ibid., p, 272.

17. Smith, *The History of the Province of New-York, Volume Two, A Continuation, 1732-1762*, p. 254.

18. Michael Kammen, *Colonial New York—A History* (New York: Charles Scriber's Sons, 1975), p. 346.

19. *The Letters and Papers of Cadwallader Colden*, Vol. VI, Collections of the New York Historical Society for the Year 1922, New York, pp. 26 and 27.

20. Edwin R. Purple, *Genealogical Notes on the Colden Family in America* (New York: Privately Printed, 1873), pp. 8 and 9.

21. Keys, *Cadwallader Colden*, p. 279.

22. *The Letters and Papers of Cadwallader Colden*, Vol. VI, p. 88.

23. *The Letters and Papers of Cadwallader Colden*, Vol. IX, Collections of the New York Historical Society for the Year 1937, New York, p. 229.

24. *The Letters and Papers of Cadwallader Colden*, Vol. VI, p. 89.

25. Keys, *Cadwallader Colden*, p. 283.

26. Smith, *The History of the Province of New-York, Volume Two, A Continuation, 1732-1762*, p. 263.

27. Ibid., p. 266.

28. "The Colden Family of Early America," http://coldenpreservation .org/ (accessed 2012).

29. *The Letters and Papers of Cadwallader Colden*, Vol. VI, pp. 213–16.

30. Ibid., p. 236.

31. Ibid., pp. 368–71.

32. Ibid., p. 381.

33. Kammen, *Colonial New York–A History*, p. 346.

34. *The Letters and Papers of Cadwallader Colden*, Vol. VI, pp. 344–47.

35. Ibid.,pp. 356–64.

36. Ibid., pp. 306 and 307.

37. Keys, *Cadwallader Colden*, p. 298.

38. Ibid., p. 338.

39. Kammen, *Colonial New York–A History*, p. 349.

40. *The Letters and Papers of Cadwallader Colden*, Vol. VII, Collections of the New York Historical Society for the Year 1923, New York, pp. 1–7.

41. Edmund S. Morgan and Helen M. Morgan, *The Stamp Act Crisis* (New York: Collier Books, 1967), pp. 314 and 315.

42. Gary B. Nash, *The Unknown American Revolution: The Unruly Birth of Democracy and the Struggle to Create America* (New York: Viking, 2005), pp. 45–47.

43. *The Letters and Papers of Cadwallader Colden*, Vol. VII, p. 56.

44. Ibid., pp. 59–62.

45. Ibid., p. 77.

46. Ibid., p. 80.

47. Ibid., p. 64.

48. Ibid., pp. 84 and 85.
49. Ibid., pp. 64 and 65.
50. Ibid., p. 67.
51. A. J. Wall, "Cadwallader Colden and His Homestead at Spring Hill, Flushing, Long Island," *Quarterly Bulletin*, VIII (1924–25), p. 12.
52. Keys, *Cadwallader Colden*, p. 325.
53. Francis R. Packard, *History of Medicine in the United States* (New York: Paul B. Hoeber, 1931), p. 505.
54. Ibid., p. 328.
55. Ibid., p. 331.
56. Ibid., pp. 333 and 334.
57. Kammen, *Colonial New York–A History*, p. 357.
58. *The Letters and Papers of Cadwallader Colden*, Vol. VII, p. 144.
59. Ibid., p. 146.

CHAPTER 7: AN OCTOGENARIAN: 1769–1776

1. *The Letters and Papers of Cadwallader Colden*, Vol. VII, Collections of the New York Historical Society for the Year 1923, New York, p. 158.
2. *The Letters and Papers of Cadwallader Colden*, Vol. IX, New York Historical Society for the Year 1937, New York, p. 218.
3. *The Letters and Papers of Cadwallader Colden*, Vol. VII, pp. 218–21.
4. Ibid., p. 348.
5. *The Letters and Papers of Cadwallader Colden*, Vol. IX, Collections of the New York Historical Society for the Year 1937, New York, p. 224.
6. Ibid., pp. 225–32.
7. *The Letters and Papers of Cadwallader Colden*, Vol. VII, pp. 173–82.
8. Alice Mapelsden Keys, *Cadwallader Colden: A Representative Eighteenth Century Official* (New York, 1906), p. 353.
9. Brooke Hindle, *The Pursuit of Science in Revolutionary America 1735-1789* (Chapel Hill: The University of North Carolina Press, 1956), p. 118.
10. *The Letters and Papers of Cadwallader Colden*, Vol. VII, p. 183.
11. Ibid., p. 186.
12. Ibid., pp. 220–22.

13. Robert Lettice Hooper to Reuben Haines, August 10, 1774, Wyck Papers, Correspondence (Philadelphia: American Philosophical Society).

14. Michael Kammen, *Colonial New York–A History* (New York: Charles Scriber's Sons, 1975), p. 363.

15. *The Letters and Papers of Cadwallader Colden*, Vol. VII, pp. 283–87.

16. Ibid., p, 273.

17. Ibid., pp. 287–90.

18. Wall, "Cadwallader Colden and His Homestead at Spring Hill, Flushing, Long Island," *Quarterly Bulletin*, VIII (1924–25), pp. 11–20.

19. Edwin R. Purple, *Genealogical Notes on the Colden Family in America* (New York: Privately Printed, 1873), p. 8.

CHAPTER 8: EPILOGUE AND LEGACY

1. Edwin R. Purple, *Genealogical Notes on the Colden Family in America* (New York: Privately Printed, 1873), pp. 110–12.

2. Ibid., p. 9.

3. Ibid.

4. A. J. Wall, "Cadwallader Colden and His Homestead at Spring Hill, Flushing, Long Island," p. 11.

5. Ibid., pp. 18 and 19. After over forty years of intermittent engagement in acquiring and studying material related to the life of Cadwallader Colden, I was surprised to learn that the location of his burial place is but two miles, as the crow flies, from the Mt. Lebanon cemetery where my parents are buried.

6. *The Letters and Papers of Cadwallader Colden*, Vol. IV, Collections of the New York Historical Society for the Year 1920, New York, p. 244.

7. *The Letters and Papers of Cadwallader Colden*, Vol. VII, Collections of the New York Historical Society for the Year 1923, New York, p. 186.

8. Ibid., pp. 305–308.

9. *The Letters and Papers of Cadwallader Colden*, Vol. V, Collections of the New York Historical Society for the Year 1921, New York, p. 13.

10. Ibid., p. 376.

11. Ibid., p. 301.

12. Cadwallader Colden, *Memoir, prepared at the request of a committee of the Common Council of the City of New York, and presented to the mayor of the city, at the celebration of the completion of the New York canals* (Printed by the order of the Corporation of New York by W. A. Davis, New York, 1825).

13. Anne MacVicar Grant, *Memoirs of an America Lady: with Sketches of Manners and Scenery in America, as They Existed Previous to the Revolution* (New York: Printed for Samuel Campbell by D. and G. Bruce, 1809), p. 6.

14. Ibid.

15. *The Letters and Papers of Cadwallader Colden*, Vol. II, Collections of the New York Historical Society for the Year 1918, New York, p. 206.

16. Lawrencec Wroth, *An America Bookshelf 1755* (Philadelphia: University of Pennsylvania Press, 1934).

17. I. Woodbridge Riley, *American Philosophy: The Early Schools* (New York: Dodd, Mead & Company, 1907), p. 329.

18. Louis I. Tucker, *Puritan Protagonist: President Thomas Clap of Yale College* (Chapel Hill: University of North Carolina Press, 1961), p. 99.

19. Max Savelle, *Seeds of Liberty: The Genesis of the American Mind* (Seattle: University of Washington Press, 1965), p. 99.

20. Adam Leroy Jones, *Early American Philosophers* (New York: Macmillan, 1898), pp. 17 and 18.

21. *The Letters and Papers of Cadwallader Colden*, Vol. I, Collections of the New York Historical Society for the Year 1917, New York, p. vii.

22. *The Letters and Papers of Cadwallader Colden*, Vol. III, p. 143.

23. *The Letters and Papers of Cadwallader Colden*, Vol. IV, Collections of the New York Historical Society for the Year 1920, New York, p. 356.

24. William Smith, Jr., *The History of the Province of New-York*, Michael Kammen, ed., (Cambridge, MA: The Belknap Press of Harvard University Press, 1972), "Introduction," p. lxx.

25. Michael Kammen, *Colonial New York: A History* (New York: Charles Scribner's Sons, 1975), p. 346.

26. V. "Biographical Memoir of Cadwallader Colden, M.D. F.R.S.," *The Monthly Recorder for June, 1813*, pp. 150 and 153.

27. V., "Biographical Memoir of Cadwallader Colden, M.D., F.R.S.," *Analectic Magazine*, IV (1814), pp. 307–312.

28. Alice Mapelsden Keys, *Cadwallader Colden: A Representative Eighteenth-Century Official* (New York, 1906), p. 365.

29. Alfred Hoermann, *Cadwallader Colden: A Figure of the American Enlightenment* (Westport, CT: Greenwood Press, 2002), p. 185.

❧ Cadwallader Colden ❧
PAPERS AND PUBLICATIONS
(LISTED CHRONOLOGICALLY
IN ORDER OF THEIR ORIGINAL WRITING,
WITH THE EXCEPTION OF TWO TRANSLATIONS)

"Animal Secretions" Presented at Royal Society of London, 1716.

"An Account of the Climate and Diseases of New York," written in early 1720s *American Medical and Philosophical Register,* I (1811): 304–310.

"A MAP of the Countrey of the FIVE Nations belonging to the province of NEW-YORK and of the LAKES near which the Nations of FAR INDIANS live with part of CANADA taken from the Map of LOUI-SIANE done by M^r De LISLE in 1718," William Bradford, New York. First published separately and in 1724 in *Colden's Papers Relating to an Act of New York for Encouragement of the Indian Trade.*

The Two Interests Reconciled: occasioned by two late Pamphlets, called The Interest of the Country and The Interest of City and Country, William Bradford, New York, 1726.

The History of the Five Nations, William Bradford, New York, 1727.

"Iliac Passion," Benjamin Franklin, Philadelphia, 1741.

"Observations on the Fever which prevailed in the City of New-York in 1741 and 2" Originally appeared in *New-York Weekly Post Boy, American Medical and Philosophical Register,* 1 (1811), p. 311.

An Explication of the First Causes of Action in Matter; and of the Cause of Gravitation, James Parker, New York, 1745.

An Explication of the First Causes of Action in Matter; and of the Cause of Gravitation, J. Brindley, London, 1745 (Pirated edition).

TRANSLATIONS

Erklärung der ersten wirkenden Ursache in der Materie, Hamburg, 1748.

Explication des premières causes de l'action dans la matière, Paris, 1751.

"An Abstract from Dr. Berkeley's Treatise on Tar-Water with Some Reflexions Thereon, Adapted to Diseases Frequent in America," New York, 1745.

"An Essay on Yellow Fever," New York, 1745.

The History of the Five Nations/Papers Relating to the Indian Trade, Thomas Osborn, London, 1747.

"Plantae Coldenghamiae in provincial Novaboracensi Americes sponte crescents, quas ad Methodem Cl, Linnaei sexulem. Anno 1742 etc. Observavit Cadwallader Colden" *Acta Societatis Regiae Scientiarum Upsalensis,* for 1743, 1749, pp. 47–82.

The Principles of Action in Matter, the Gravitation of Bodies and the Motion of Planets, explained those Principles, Robert Dodsley, London, 1751.

"The Cure of Cancer" (Pokeweed), *Gentleman's Magazine,* 21 (1751), pp. 305–308 and 22; (1752), p. 302.

Letter to Dr. John Fothergill "Concerning the Throat-Distemper," *Medical Observations and Inquiries,* London, 1753.

Treatise on Wounds and Fevers, New York, 1765.

✧ REFERENCES ✧

The *Aberdeen Magazine for the year XDCCLXI*. Aberdeen, Scotland, 1761.

American National Biography. Vol. 5. Oxford and New York, Oxford University Press, 1999.

Bell, Whitfield J., Jr. *Patriot Improvers: Biographical Sketches of Members of the American Philosophical Society*, Vol. 1, Philadelphia, American Philosophical Society, 1997.

Berkeley, Edmund and Dorothy Smith Berkeley. *Dr. Alexander Garden of Charles Town*. Chapel Hill: University of North Carolina Press, 1969.

————. *Dr. John Mitchell*. Chapel Hill: The University of North Carolina Press, 1974.

————. *The Correspondence of John Bartram 1734-1777*. Gainesville: University of Florida Press, 1992.

Blau, Joseph L. *Men and Movements in American Philosophy*. New York: Prentice-Hall, 1952.

Britten, James. "Biographical Notes. VIII—Jan Colden and the Flora of New York," *Journal of Botany, British and Foreign*, 33 (1895), pp. 12–15.

Bullock, Charles J. "Introduction: Life and Writings of William Douglass." In "A Discourse Concerning the Currencies of the British Plantations in America &c. by William Douglass," edited by Charles J. Bullock, *Economic Studies* (Journal of the American Economic Association), 2, no. 5, Google Books.

Clearwater, Alphonso T., ed. *The History of Ulster County New York*. Westminster, MD: Clearwater, Heritage Book Facsimile, 2007.

Colden, Cadwallader. "To His Excellency Brigadier Hunter Governor of New York, January 16, 1719/20, *Copy Book of Letters on Subjects of Philosophy, Medicine, Friendship, 1716–1721*. Colden MS., New York Historical Society, unpaginated.

————. *The History of the Five Indian Nations*. Ithaca, New York; Cornell University Press, 1958.

————. "Observations on the Situation, Soil, Climate, Water, Communications, Boundaries, etc. of the Province of New York, (1738)" in E. B. O'Callaghan *Documents Relative to the Colonial History of New York, Albany, 1856-57.*

_____. "Observations on the Fever which prevailed in the City of New-York in 1741 and 2, written in 1743," *American Medical and Philosophical Reporter,* 1, 1811.

_____. "Plantae Coldenghamiae in provincial Novaboracnesi Americes sponte crescents, quas ad Methodem Cl. Linnaei sexulem. Anno 1742 etc. Observavit et descripsit Cadwallader Colden," *Acta Societatis Regiae Scientiarum Upsalinsis* for 1743, 1749.

_____. "Of the First Principles of Morality or the Actions of Intelligent Beings," Manuscript I, Rosenbach Museum and Library, Philadelphia.

_____. *Memoir, prepared at the request of a committee of the Common Council of the City of New York, and presented to the mayor of the city, at the celebration of the completion of the New York canals.* New York: Printed by the order of the Corporation of New York by W. A. Davis, 1825.

"The Colden Family of Early America," http://coldenpreservation.org/

Collections of the New-York Historical Society for the Years 1917–1923, 1934, 1935: *The Letters and Papers of Cadwallader Colden,* 9 Volumes. Collections of the New-York Historical Society for the Years 1917–1923, 1934, 1935: New York, Printed for the New York Historical Society.

"Criticism of *The Principles of the Action in Matter,*" unpublished translation of Kastner's remarks, Colden MSS, New York Historical Society.

Darlington, W. *Memorials of John Bartram and Humphry Marhsall.* Philadelphia, 1849, p. 195.

Denny, Margaret. "Linnaeus and his Disciple in Carolina: Alexander Garden." *Isis,* 38 (1948), p. 173.

Devine, Joseph. "Cadwallader Colden: Father of the American Canal System." http://home.roadrunner.com/-montghistory/ (accessed 2012).

Dictionary of National Biography, Vol. 4. Oxford: Oxford University Press, 1964.

Douglass, William. *A Summary, Historical and Political, of the . . . British Settlements in North-America.* 2 vols., London: R. and J. Dodsley, 1760, p. 106.

Garden to Ellis, December 16, 1765, James Edward Smith (ed.). *A Selection of the Correspondence of Linnaeus and Other Naturalists,* Vol I, London: Longman, Hurst, Rees, Orme and Brown, 1821.

Gitlin, Louis L. "Cadwallader Colden as Scientist and Philosopher." *New York History* 16 (1935), p. 175.

Grant, Alexander. *The Story of the University of Edinburgh,* Vol. 1, London: Longmans, Green, 1884.

Grant, Anne MacVicar. *Memoirs of an America Lady: with Sketches of Manners and Scenery in America, as They Existed Previous to the Revolution.* New York: Printed for Samuel Campbell by D. and G. Bruce, 1809.

Haley, Jacquetta M. "Farming on the Hudson Valley frontier: Cadwallader Colden's farm journal 1717-1736." *Hudson Valley Regional Review* 6 (March 1989), p. 2.

Hindle, Brooke. "Cadwallader Colden's Extension of the Newtonian Principles." *The William and Mary Quarterly,* Third Series, 13, no. 4 (1956), pp. 464 and 465.

_____. *The Pursuit of Science in Revolutionary America 1735-1789.* Chapel Hill: The University of North Carolina Press, 1956.

Histoire de L'Amerique septentrionale pr Mr. de Bacqueville de la Potherie. Paris: L. Nion et F. Didot, 1722.

Hoermann, Alfred R. *Cadwallader Colden: A Figure of the American Enlightenment.* Westport, CT: Greenwood Press, 2002.

Huske, John. *The Present State of North America.* London: R. and J. Dodsley, 1755.

Jarcho, Saul. "John Mitchell, Benjamin Rush and Yellow Fever." *Bulletin of the History of Medicine* XXXI (1957), pp. 132–36.

Jones, Adam Leroy. *Early American Philosophers.* New York Macmillan, 1898.

Kammen, Michael. *Colonial New York–A History.* New York: Charles Scriber's Sons, 1975.

Kerkhonen, Martin. *Peter Kalm's North American Journey: Its Ideological Background and Results.* Helsinki: The Finnish Historical Society, 1959.

Keys, Alice Mapelsden. *Cadwallader Colden: A Representative Eighteenth Century Official.* New York, 1906.

Lahontan, Mr. Baron de. *Nouveaux Voyages de Mr.Baron de Lahontan Dans L'Amerique Septentrionale.* La Haye: Chez les Freres l Honore, 1702.

Lamb, Martha J. *History of the City of New York: Its Origins, Rise and Progress,* Vol. I. New York: A. S. Barnes and Company, 1877.

McVickar, John. *A Domestic Narrative of the Life of Samuel Bard, M.D.: LL.D Late President of the College of Physicians and Surgeons of the University of the State of New York*, New York, 1822.

Miller Collection. "S. Griffin to Levi Bartlett [April 4, 1794]." Richmond, Virginia Academy of Medicine.

Mitchell, D. D. Jo. "Dissertatio Brevis de Principiis Botanicorum et Zoologorum desque novo stabilende naturae rerum congruo cum Appendice Aliquot Generum plantarum recens conditorum . . ." *Acta Physico-Medica Academiae Caesarae . . . Ephemerides VIII*, 1748.

Mitchell, John. "An Essay upon the Causes of the Different Colours of People in different Climates." *Philosophical Transactions* XLIII (1744), pp. 102–150.

Morgan, Edmund S. and Helen M. Morgan. *The Stamp Act Crisis*. New York: Collier Books, 1967.

Nash, Gary B. *The Unknown American Revolution: The Unruly Birth of Democracy and the Struggle to Create America*. New York: Viking, 2005.

Newton, Sir Isaac. *Mathematical Principles of Natural Philosophy*, ed. by Florian Cajori from the 1737 edition, Berkeley: University of California Press, 1946.

O'Callaghan, Edmund B. *The Documentary History of the State of New York*. Albany, NY, 1849–1851, Vol. I.

_____., ed., *Documents Relative to the Colonial History of New York*. Albany, 1856–1857.

O'Neill, Jean, and Elizabeth P. McLean. *Petyer Collinson and the Eighteenth-Century Natural History Exchange*. Philadelphia: American Philosophical Society, 2008.

Packard, Francis R. *History of Medicine in the United States*, Vol. 1, New York: Paul B. Hoeber, 1931.

Pratt, Scott L. and John Ryder, eds., *The Philosophical Writings of Cadwallader Colden*. Amherst, NY: Prometheus Books, 2002.

Purple, Edwin R. *Genealogical Notes on the Colden Family*. Private printing, 1873.

Rickett, H. W., and E. C.Hall., eds., *Botanic Manuscript of Jane Colden*. New York: Garden Club of Orange and Dutchess Counties, 1963, p. 53.

Riley, I. Woodbridge. *American Philosophy: The Early Schools*. New York: Dodd, Mead & Company, 1907.

Robbins, Paula Ivaska. *Jane Colden: America's First Woman Botanist.* New York: Fleischmanns, Purple Mountain Press, 2009.

Ross, Shelley. *Fall From Grace.* New York: Random House, 1958.

Schwartz, Seymour I. *The French and Indian War 1754–1763.* New York: Simon & Schuster, 1994.

Schwartz, Seymour I. and Ralph E. Ehrenberg. *The Mapping of America.* New York: Harry N. Abrams, 1980.

Sevelle, Max. *Seeds of Liberty: The Genesis of the American Mind.* New York: A. A. Knopf, 1948.

Shryock, Richard Harrison. *Medicine and Society in America 1660–1680.* New York: New York University Press, 1972.

Smith, William, Jr. *The History of the Province of New-York . . . to the Year MDC-CXXXII.* London, 1757, Vol. I, Michael Kammen, ed., Cambridge, MA: The Belknap Press of Harvard University Press, 1972.

Stearns, Raymond Phineas. *Science in the British Colonies of America.* Urbana: University of Illinois Press, 1970.

Stookey, Bryon Polk. *A History of Colonial Medical Education in the Province of New York with Its Subsequent Development.* Springfield, IL: Charles C. Thomas, 1961.

Thatcher, Herbert. "Dr. Mitchell, M.D., F.R.S. of Virginia." *Virginia Magazine of History and Biography* 40 (1932).

Tolles, Frederick B. *James Logan and the Culture of Provincial America.* Boston: Little, Brown and Co., 1957.

Toner, Joseph M. *Contributions to the Annals of Medical Progress and medical education in the United States before and during the war of independence.* Washington, DC: Government Printing Office, 1874.

Tucker, Louis I. *Puritan Protagonist: President Thomas Clap of Yale College.* Chapel Hill: University of North Carolina Press, n.d.

V. "Biographical Memoir of Cadwallader Colden, M.D. F. R. S." *Monthly Recorder for June* (1813), pp. 150 and 153.

_____. "Biographical Memoir of Cadwallader Colden, M.D., F. R. S.," *Analectic Magazine* IV (1814): 307–312.

Vail, Ann Murray. "Jane Colden, An Early New York Botanist." *Torreya* 7 (1907), p. 32.

Wadsworth, Alice Colden. "Sketch of the Colden and Murray Families" (1819), Manuscript Division, New York Public Library, quoted in Alfred R. Hoermann, *Cadwallader Colden: A Figure of the American Enlightenment.* Westport, CT: Greenwood Press, 2002.

Wall, A. J. "Cadwallader Colden and His Homestead at Spring Hill, Flushing, Long Island." *Quarterly Bulletin* VIII (1924–25), p. 12.

Wroth, Lawrence C. *An American Bookshelf 1755.* Philadelphia: University of Pennsylvania Press, 1934.

Wyck Papers, Correspondence. American Philosophical Society, Philadelphia.

✑ INDEX ✑